MEMBERS IN PARTICULAR

A Comparison of the Physical Body with the Body of Christ

Janet M. Magiera

LWM Publications
Light of the Word Ministry
San Diego, California

Abbreviations

All verses listed are quoted from the King James Version unless otherwise noted by parentheses after the verse citation.

ESV: English Standard Version, Crossways Bibles, 2007.

MGI: Aramaic Peshitta New Testament Translation, LWM Publications, 2006.

NASB: New American Standard Bible, The Lockman Foundation, 1977.

Illustrations are utilized form Smartdraw 2009, Healthcare Edition, www.smartdraw.com.

Table of Contents

Introduction

THE BODY OF CHRIST

The Church today is described as the Body of Christ. The metaphor is simply stated in I Corinthians 12:27: "Now ye are the body of Christ, and members in particular." Biblically, the physical body is an illustration of the practical application of the members of the Church living together in harmony and with integration.

This book is a comparison of the Church with the physical body and is an explanation of the validity of that analogy. It is about how we are individual members of the Church and what our relationships are with each other. The intricacies of the physical body will give us many clues to the God-inspired design of the Body of Christ. The way that God designed the human form and how it meshes together is so beautiful that after putting a microscope to its details, it only serves to bring awe to see the magnificence of our heavenly Father. In that examination we can see how perfect his illustration is to help us to understand how the Body of Christ works together.

As in every analogy or illustration used in the Bible, we need to be careful not to assume that every aspect of the comparison is applicable, otherwise the illustration will be pushed too far. However, as you will see, there are so many clear comparisons that it is not necessary to allegorize every single aspect of the physical body. In this book, I distinguish the physical body with small capital letters from the Body of Christ in capital letters. This will help us to see the analogy.

INTRODUCTION

What is the Body of Christ and how does it function? Who are the members in particular and how are they supposed to relate to each other? In order to begin to answer these questions the first point we must keep in mind is that the image of the Body of Christ as the Church cannot be considered separately from our Lord Jesus Christ.

Colossians 1:18:
He is the head of the body, the church....

Christ as the head of the Body is more than a local community of faith. It is a unique tie to the risen and glorified physical body of Jesus Christ. And the saving power of the resurrection is the key to the integral unity of those who confess Jesus as Lord and believe that God raised him from the dead (Romans 10:9, 10). A body cannot function without a head, just as the physical body is dead without life in the brain to coordinate and guide it.

The unity of the Body as a whole entity being joined to Christ is the foundational concept of the Church. This is succinctly stated in the entry in the *Dictionary of Biblical Imagery* under "body": "It is the believers' unity with Christ which creates the fellowship, not the fellowship which creates the unity with Christ."[1] This intrinsic unity can never be ignored. We must always consider every aspect of the illustration in this light.

The second point to remember as these chapters unfold is that the way that I am presenting this illustration is in snapshots. The organization of the physical body shows us different aspects of how the Body of Christ functions. So when we look at the cells,

---

[1] *Dictionary of Biblical Imagery*, p. 109.

we see one comparison. When we look at tissues, we see another, and so forth. The aspects are not exclusive of each other, but they are as if we took a camera photo of the subject from different angles. Also, I am not trained in the medical field and do not pretend to know the details that someone with that background would understand.

This book is a comparison of the physical body with the Body of Christ and is an explanation of the beauty of that analogy. It is about how we are individual members of the Church and what our relationships are with each other. Each chapter is designed in order to provoke thoughtful consideration of the comparisons. It is my prayer that "the eyes of our hearts would be enlightened" (Ephesians 1:18, Aramaic translation) and filled with understanding as we examine this wonderful topic.

Chapter 1

THE MYSTERY OF THE ONE BODY

I Corinthians 12:12:
For as the body is one, and hath many members, and all the members of that one body, being many, are one body: so also is Christ.

Being members in the Body of Christ means that we are involved together in a mystery that God hid as a secret from everyone. It was not until after Jesus Christ was raised from the dead and ascended to the right hand of God that the mystery was finally revealed.

I Corinthians 2:7 (MGI):
but we speak the wisdom of God in a mystery, which was hidden and [which] God determined beforehand, from before the ages, for our glory.

THE MYSTERY REVEALED

The Body of Christ was God's mystery, the secret that was "hid from ages and generations" (Colossians 1:26) and "which was kept secret since the world began" (Romans 16:25). Prior to this revealing, all of the blessings of God were given to the descendants of Abraham through Isaac and Jacob, who are called the Judeans or Jews. If Gentiles wanted to be a part of the covenant God made with the Judeans, then they needed to become proselytes and convert to Judaism. Even after the day of Pentecost when the first believers were born again, the

4

outpouring of the gift of Holy Spirit was still limited to Judeans who believed that Jesus was the Messiah.

But then during the ministry of the apostle Paul, the mystery was revealed and not only included the Gentiles, but made them an integral part of a totally new entity called the "new man" in Ephesians.

Ephesians 2:13-18:
But now in Christ Jesus ye who sometimes were far off [the Gentiles] are made nigh by the blood of Christ.
For he is our peace, who hath made both [Jews and Gentiles] one, and hath broken down the middle wall of partition between us;
Having abolished in his flesh the enmity, even the law of commandments contained in ordinances; for to make in himself of twain one new man, so making peace;
And that he might reconcile both unto God in one body by the cross, having slain the enmity thereby:
And came and preached peace to you which were afar off, [Gentiles] and to them that were nigh [Jews].
For through him we both have access by one Spirit unto the Father.

What brought the Jews and Gentiles together was the access to the Father by the same Spirit. No longer was there a distinction between the two groups, but they became "one new man."

Ephesians 3:6 further clarifies the mystery in a nutshell:

Ephesians 3:6:
That the Gentiles should be fellowheirs, and of the same body, and partakers of his promise in Christ by the gospel.

In order to get an understanding of this verse, first of all, we need to note two figures of speech in the Greek. One is *polysyndeton*, which is the multiple use of "ands", which sets apart and emphasizes each of the three phrases. Each phrase needs to have the most deliberate attention. The other figure of speech is *homeopropheron*, or alliteration, "the repetition of the same letter or syllable at the commencement of successive words."[2] The words "fellowheirs," "of the same body" and "partakers" each begin with the Greek word *sun* or variations of *sun*: *sunkeronomos*, *sussomos*, and *summetochos*, respectively. *Sun* means "with, in conjunction with, united with, together in, something common to both, implying fellowship, union or agreement with."[3] What is emphasized by the alliteration is "together with, united with."

Now let us look at the three distinct phrases. The Gentiles are fellow-heirs, "together-heirs" with whom? The only other place this word in Ephesians 3:6 for fellow-heirs is used is in Romans and is translated "joint-heirs."

Romans 8:17a:
And if children, then heirs; heirs of God, and joint-heirs with Christ;

Both Jews and Gentiles who are born again are joint-heirs with Christ. The mystery revealed is that both Jews and Gentiles would share fully in the inheritance with Christ. This first phrase emphasizes that the Church is a family with God as their Father and with all the rights and privileges of sons.

---

[2] Bullinger, E.W., *Figures of Speech Used in the Bible*, p. 171, 208.
[3] Bullinger, E.W., *A Critical Lexicon and Concordance to the English and Greek New Testament*, p. 888.

The Gentiles are "of the same body" as whom?

Romans 12:5:
So we, being many, are one body in Christ, and everyone members one of another.

We are of the same Body with Christ. It is Christ's Body. The mystery revealed is that both Jews and Gentiles are inseparably linked with Christ as a unified whole, functioning together with him as the head. This is the second illustration used of the Church, that we are a Body. It portrays how we practically live in our relationship with each other and with God and with Christ.

The Gentiles are "partakers" with whom?

I Corinthians 10:16b, 17:
...the bread which we break, is it not the communion of the body of Christ?
For we being many are one bread, and one body; for we are all partakers of that one bread.

The "one bread" represents Christ's flesh and all that he accomplished in his flesh. We are partakers with Christ and all that he accomplished. This is being identified with Christ.

Romans 6:3, 4:
Know ye not, that so many of us as were baptized into Jesus Christ were baptized into his death?
Therefore we are buried with him by baptism into death: that like as Christ was raised up from the dead by the glory of the Father, even so we also should walk in newness of life.

That means that when he died, we died with him. When he arose, we arose with him. The mystery revealed is that we have a full sharing in all that Christ accomplished and the salvation he made available.

In Ephesians 3:6 the word "partakers" is *summetochos* and according to Moulton-Milligan, this Greek word was used in the business documents called papyri in the sense of a joint ownership, "joint possessors of a house."[4] The holding we have in joint ownership is the gift of the full measure of the Spirit and by that we are partakers of Christ.

But what is the "house" of which we are "joint-possessors"? This is explained in Ephesians that we are the temple of God and his habitation.

Ephesians 2:20b-22:
...Jesus Christ himself being the chief corner <u>stone</u>;
In whom all the building fitly framed together groweth unto a holy temple in the Lord:
In whom ye also are builded together for an habitation of God through the Spirit.

Hebrews 3:14:
For we are made partakers of Christ...

Hebrews 6:4:
...and have tasted of the heavenly gift, and were made partakers of the Holy Ghost,

---

[4] Milligan, G. and Moulton, J.H. *Vocabulary of the Greek New Testament*, p. 406.

We are partakers of God's habitation in Christ by the Spirit. This dwelling place of God is where we are seated (Ephesians 2:6). All the power and rest which was made available in Christ is ours together with him by way of the Spirit. The intimate fellowship and worship of God is ours also. This is being partakers of his promise in Christ.

IN CHRIST

Ephesians 3:6:
That the Gentiles should be fellowheirs, and of the same body, and partakers of his promise in Christ by the gospel.

All three of these phrases emphasize being united with, or in conjunction with Christ. In Ephesians 3:6, the phrase "in Christ" is immediately following "promise", but rather than only belonging to the last phrase, it belongs to all three phrases. The Gentiles are fellow-heirs with Christ, of the same Body with Christ and partakers of God's promise in Christ. Robertson, in *The Expositor's Greek New Testament*, describes "in Christ by the gospel" succinctly as follows:

These words are best taken as qualifying all the three former terms. The jointheirship, membership, and participation had their objective ground and reason in Christ Jesus, and were made the actual possession of these Gentiles by the medium or agency of the Gospel that was preached to them.[5]

---

[5] Nicoll, W. Robertson, *The Expositor's Greek New Testament*, p. 305.

THE MYSTERY OF THE ONE BODY

It was in Christ that the mystery was unfolded. We who formerly were Jews or Gentiles are now joint-heirs with Christ! We are of Christ's Body! We share fully in all that Christ accomplished!

This unique fellowship can be seen even more vividly by a study of the structure of Ephesians 3:6.

Ephesians 3:5, 6:
Which in other ages was not made known unto the sons of men, as it is now revealed unto his holy apostles and prophets by the Spirit; That the Gentiles should be fellowheirs, and of the same body, and partakers of his promise in Christ by the gospel:

The last phrase "by the Spirit" of Ephesians 3:5 parallels "in Christ" in verse 6. Charles Welch in his book, *The Testimony of the Lord's Prisoner*, describes the structure in the following way as an alternation that is like a "sandwich":[6]

>   A) now revealed to holy apostles and prophets
>   B) by (in) the Spirit
>   C) fellow heirs
>   C) of the same body
>   C) partakers of his promise
>   B) in Christ
>   A) by the gospel

He then elaborates that the mystery is:

bounded by the terms 'in Spirit' and 'in Christ' and has a three-fold equality, a fellowship without precedent.... The words 'in Spirit' of verse 5 do not refer to the revelation made to the apostles

---

[6] Welch, Charles, *The Testimony of the Lord's Prisoner*, p. 82.

and prophets, but, as at the end of Ephesians ii, indicate the only sphere in which such an equality is possible.[7]

It is by or in the Spirit that we are "together with" Christ. The gift of the Holy Spirit is the "something common" which links us inseparably together in Christ.

I Corinthians 12: 12, 13:
For as the body is one, and hath many members, and all the members of that one body, being many, are one body: so also is Christ.
For by one Spirit are we all baptized into one body, whether we be Jews or Gentiles, whether we be bond or free; and have been all made to drink into one Spirit.

We are "of the same body" with Christ for we are all baptized by one Spirit. This is the unique tie that binds the Body of Christ together–we each have the exact same gift of Holy Spirit! That is what makes us one.

I Corinthians 6:17:
But he that is joined unto the Lord is one spirit.

Ephesians 3:6 is the great mystery revealed in a nutshell. It is a summary of three major points which we have by the Spirit and in Christ. "By the Spirit" is the something common which unites both Gentile and Judean. "In Christ" is with whom we are united and how and why we have this union. We are fellow-heirs in Christ and are part of the great family and household of God, entitled to a full inheritance. We are one Body in Christ and are thus a unified functioning whole. We are partakers together in

---

[7] *Ibid.*, p. 88.

Christ, sharing fully in all that he accomplished and all that he has and will have. We are of the household of God, of the Body of Christ and are the habitation of God. This is the mystery which **was** secret, but is "now revealed"!

MEMBERS IN PARTICULAR

The mystery revealed is that we are "of the same body" as we have seen from Ephesians 3:6. The Church of the New Testament is compared to a "body," called the Body of Christ. Here are several verses where the illustration is explicitly stated as a metaphor–the Church **is** the Body:

> *I Corinthians 12:27:*
> *Now ye are the body of Christ, and members in particular.*

> *Ephesians 1:22, 23:*
> *And hath put all things under his feet, and gave him to be the head over all things to the church,*
> *Which is his body, the fulness of him that filleth all in all.*

> *Colossians 1:18a:*
> *And he is the head of the body, the church....*

The specific meaning of the term body refers to physical life: "the whole physical structure and substance of a man, animal, or plant" but can be used generally as a "group of people or things regarded as a unit."[8] Although believers in Christ are definitely a group of persons organized as a unit, the way the Bible uses the phrase "Body of Christ" is specifically referring to the comparison

---

[8] *Webster's New World Dictionary of the American Language*, p. 163.

of an organized structure of physical life, and more specifically, the human body. Therefore it is important to understand that when the Bible uses the term "body" figuratively or discusses parts of the body, it is a comparison of the physical human body to the spiritual Body of Christ.

The body is one unit, an integral being, but it has many parts or "particulars" that comprise it. We all have the same Spirit within when we become born-again, but God clearly loves diversity and has made us all unique. He is able to work in each of us as members in particular because of our part in the Body as a whole.

The Greek word for "in particular" in I Corinthians 12:27 means, "one of the constituent parts of a whole."[9] If you are a particular member in the whole Body, then you have a particular place.

I Corinthians 12:27 (MGI):
Now you are the body of Christ and members in your place.

By viewing how we are members in particular in the Body of Christ, we will be able to share fully and live the mystery that is now revealed. We share in all that Christ accomplished for us and we share in his Body, living as a whole unit **together.**

---

[9] *The New Thayer's Greek-English Lexicon of the New Testament*, p. 400.

Chapter 2

PARTICULAR CELLS

The human body is categorized in science into four main parts: cells, tissues, organs and systems. The smallest unit is the cell. Similar cells join together to form tissues. Groups of tissues form organs and combinations of organs form systems. We will be examining each of these categories to see the comparisons with the spiritual Body of Christ. But we need to start with the basic unit, the cell.

THE CELL

The individual is like a cell. Each cell has several common parts no matter what kind of cell it is or what it does. It has a nucleus, protoplasm and a membrane. The nucleus can be compared to Spirit, the protoplasm can be compared to the soul and the membrane to the body. The membrane is the way things are passed in and out of the cell. Through various processes (such as diffusion) nutrients and ingredients that the cell needs are allowed into the cell. These compare to the five senses that are the "processes" whereby the human body receives information.

The protoplasm is the liquid substance inside the cell. It is the medium in which things occur in the cell and there are specific parts within this protoplasm that have to do with the kind of cell it is. Similarly, the soul of an individual has many things in common with other human beings, but the specific parts have to do with the special combination of heredity and development for that individual. And even though there are individuals who are very similar to each other just as there are kinds of cells that are alike, no two cells in the human body are

exactly the same. Each one is unique and functions as a single unit. In fact, there are over 6 billion cells in the human body, but each one is unique!

The nucleus is the carrier for all of the DNA and chromosomes for the cell. The human body has 46 chromosomes, 23 from the mother's egg and 23 from the father's sperm. These are the blueprints for reproduction and are the same in every cell. The only cells that do not have 46 chromosomes are the sperm and egg cells. These each have only 23, so that when they are joined, they will have 46 chromosomes. The nucleus can be compared to the Holy Spirit which is given to each individual in order for them to be in the Body of Christ. It is the blueprint, if you will, of the "full measure of the stature of the fullness of Christ" (Ephesians 2:15).

I Corinthians 12:13:
For by one Spirit are we all baptized into one body, whether we be Jews or Gentiles, whether we be bond or free; and have been all made to drink into one Spirit.

Every believer in the spiritual Body of Christ is given the full measure of the gift of the Holy Spirit that was in Jesus Christ. The spiritual power is the same in every individual. One cell does not have more chromosomes than another cell. So no believer has more of the gift of the Holy Spirit than any other believer. That is such a blessing to understand when thinking of the Church. The believer who has just this hour been born again has the full complement of Holy Spirit, just as much as the believer who has been in the Body of Christ for 70 years. Certainly there are points to make about growing up in Christ and the maturity that an individual develops in his life, but this basic truth is very important to keep in mind when we view each other in the Body of Christ.

There are seven main kinds of cells. The truths about the kinds of cells will help us to see that each individual in the Body of Christ functions in groups of "kinds." These are not the only kinds of cells in the body, but as we will see in the next chapter, these seven kinds of cells line up with the seven main functions in the Church. There are epithelial or glandular cells, red blood cells, white cells, fat cells, nerve cells, muscle cells, and connective cells. The following shows simplified pictures of the different kinds of cells:

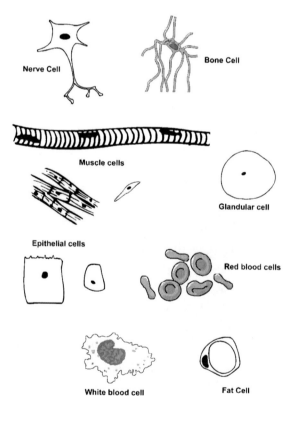

Nerve Cell

Bone Cell

Muscle cells

Glandular cell

Epithelial cells

Red blood cells

White blood cell

Fat Cell

As you can see, cells come in many shapes and sizes. That certainly is true of the Body of Christ and of the human population as a whole. Beyond the obvious differences in physical characteristics, there are specific functions that each kind of cell performs, and their shape and characteristics are specifically designed for that function. This becomes crucial to understand in the comparison with the spiritual Body of Christ. Let us take a closer look at the kinds of cells and how they do their jobs.

Epithelial cells are sometimes called glandular cells or mucous membrane cells. They are found in many parts of the body. They form the whole skin covering and line the mouth, throat, nose, esophagus and the inside of every major organ. Below is a picture of small portion of skin. The shape of the epithelial cells vary from short to elongated, and the epithelium has several layers on the outside.

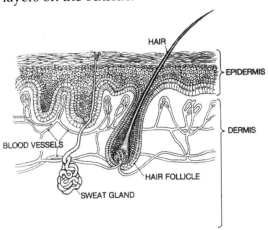

This design is so that it can filter out unnecessary and unwanted things from other cells. For example, in the lungs, the mucous membrane cells help to carry excess mucous and bacteria from the air and expel it to the surface to allow it to be carried away as waste. When we get a cold, the bacteria or virus causes an infection and an abundant production of mucous. The membrane cells are hard-pressed to take care of all of the excess, hence the sneezing, coughing and runny noses. When the mucous membrane cells are functioning properly, they are able to handle the pollutants that come into our bodies from the air and our food and expel them as waste. The skin works in the same fashion as a protector from outside bacteria, but also as a way for the body to expel unwanted things. Sweating is a process that helps to eliminate things that have come up to the surface of the epithelial cells.

Epithelial cells are crucial to the functioning of the body as we have explained. What is important to see is that they are positioned everywhere in the body. In the comparison with the spiritual Body of Christ, many believers question where they should be at any given time and are constantly asking if they should move and go to this location or that. Sometimes there is clear direction about a move to a certain place, but more often, it does not matter **where** a believer is, as far as location, as much as **how** he is functioning. You can take an epithelial cell from the nose and put it in the stomach and it will function just fine.

This is important to understand in light of the passage in I Corinthians 12 that talks about the members (cells) of the Body.

I Corinthians 12:18-20:
But now hath God set the members every one of them in the body, as it hath pleased him.
And if they were all one member, where were the body?
But now are they many members, yet but one body.

The physical body is made up of many cells and they each function according to the kind of cell they are. If they were all the same kind of cell, how would the body function? The same question applies to the Church. If each person in the Church were the same, how would the Church function?

Let us look a little more closely at some of the other kinds of cells. The following is a picture of a motor nerve cell:

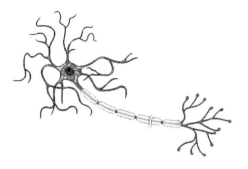

Observe how different it looks from the epithelial cell pictured before. Have you ever felt that there are some people that you just naturally "hit it off" with and others that you don't understand the least bit about, even in the Body of Christ? Well, that has something to do with the fact that cells that are alike gravitate to other cells of the same kind. That is natural in a very good sense, because cells that join together then can form tissues and organs.

Nerve cells are the sensory communicators in the body. They link together to form long chains of networks from the brain to the spinal cord and throughout the whole body. As an example, I never appreciated how important these chains were until my first son was born. During the delivery, the nurses tried to put an I.V. in my leg. It ended up severing a nerve connection in the surface of my leg and for about six months afterward I had no feeling in the whole top part of my left thigh. Gradually the feeling was restored and the nerves were healed to connect together again. But it was a strange feeling not to have sensation in that part of the leg.

COMPARISON OF CELLS

One of the things that happens in the Body of Christ is that Christians compare themselves to each other, often critically. In some cases, there are only mild observations, but at other times Christians can be very judgmental. If we applied this principle of understanding that there are different kinds of cells in the body and each kind is crucial to the whole of the body working together, then perhaps we would stop judging each other negatively because of our differences.

Another thing that happens when we do this kind of comparison is that we say that we have no need of different kinds of members than we perceive that we are.

I Corinthians 12:22-23:
Nay, much more those members of the body, which seem to be more feeble, are necessary:
And those members of the body, which we think to be less honourable, upon these we bestow more abundant honour; and our uncomely parts have more abundant comeliness.

Whichever kind of member (or cell) you think is less honorable, that is the one on which you should bestow more abundant honor.

Fat cells are a good example of this principle because they look fairly nondescript. Despite how they look, without fat cells in the body, we would not have any energy or any place to draw energy from whenever we wanted to do the simplest activity. It is in the fat cells that the body stores nutrients needed to provide energy. There are fat cell depots that are like giant warehouses for the release of energy. There are fat cells coming in and out of the depots at all times. Fat cells serve as cushions around your internal organs and also carry some essential vitamins to cells that need them. We need fat cells!

As you can see, the first point mentioned in the discussion about epithelial cells applies to each kind, including fat cells. These kinds of cells that we have been discussing are found throughout the body and could be moved from one place to another and still perform their specific functions. This principle is illustrated in burn victims when skin is grafted from some other place on the body to replace the burned area. This further point about the perception of each member in the Body towards each other is summed up at the end of I Corinthians 12:

I Corinthians 12:24-27:
For our comely parts have no need: but God hath tempered the body together, having given more abundant honour to that part which lacked:
That there should be no schism in the body; but that the members should have the same care one for another.
And whether one member suffer, all the members suffer with it; or one member be honoured, all the members rejoice with it.

PARTICULAR CELLS

Now ye are the body of Christ, and members in particular.

I challenge you to determine to care for the person whom you understand and relate to the least, and see the way that they manifest the Spirit of God in their life. If we honor the part that we think lacks, then we will start to care one for another. Rejoice that we are all "members in particular." Then and only then will there be no schism in the Body of Christ.

As you can see from this chapter, we have been discussing verses that use the word "member." In all of the uses of this word, you can substitute in your mind the word "cell" for "member" and the passages come alive. All of the passages are either talking about the individual body or the Body of Christ.

Chapter 3

FUNCTIONS IN THE BODY

Despite the fact that God designed the Body of Christ to function together, there are thousands of denominations in Christianity with further splits and schisms forming all the time. Why does this division happen so often and what can we do about it? I believe that this chapter will help us find an answer to these puzzling questions. The answer comes in understanding how cells function together. In a medical explanation of the body, when cells join together, they form tissues.

The following is a picture of what muscle cells look like in a cross section of tissue.

There are actually three different kinds of muscle cells. Those pictured above are the striated muscle cells. They come together to form the voluntary muscles, ones that are controlled by our will. Another kind are smooth muscle cells, for example ones that line the esophagus. These are involuntary. The heart has another particular kind of muscle cell that is also involuntary. Every kind of cell has many variations and there are also many specialized cells.

In this chapter we will examine the seven major kinds of tissue and the functions they perform. They line up with the various "gifts" that are mentioned in Romans 12. The verses quoted from Romans 12 are from the *Aramaic Peshitta New Testament Translation*.

Romans 12:4:
For as in one body we have many members and all members do not have one function,

The Aramaic word for "function" is *suerana* and can be translated in a variety of ways, including business, deed, office, opportunity, performance, fact. Its root verb means to perform something. I think that "business" is a good translation and helps to explain what function is. Every member does not have the same business.

The next verse goes on to point out that we are members of one another.

Romans 12:5:
So also we who are many are one body in Christ and each one of us are members of one another.

Even though this passage is describing specific "business" that members are doing, it is important to keep in mind that all the business is interconnected. This can be very vividly seen when we look at the comparison with the physical cells.

Romans 12:6-8:
But we have different gifts according to the grace that is given to us. There is [the gift] of prophecy (according to the measure of one's faith),
and there is [the gift] of ministering one has in his ministering,
and there is [the gift] of a teacher in his teaching,
and there is [the gift] of a comforter in his comforting, and [there is the gift] of one who gives, with simplicity, and [there is the gift] of one who leads, with diligence, and [there is the gift] of one who is merciful, with cheerfulness.

The next thing to note about this passage is that there are seven "gifts" mentioned. The first four are not qualified with any descriptions. The last three are listed with various qualifications of how to perform the job. "In the case of the first four gifts the exhortation is concerned with the sphere in which the gift is to be exercised but in the case of the last three it is directed to the disposition of heart and will with which the service is to be rendered."[10]

You can also see from the Aramaic translation that there are words in brackets. These words are added so that the text can make sense in English and here they are indicating a figure of speech called *ellipsis*. One could actually put in the whole phrase "there is the gift according to the grace that is given to us", which is from verse 6, in every place where there are brackets. The use of the figure of speech *ellipsis* always emphasizes the words that

---

[10] Murray, John. *The New International Commentary on the New Testament*, p. 127.

are missing. So what we are to remember here is that these actions are always according to the grace that is given us.

The word "gifts" is used to describe the major functions in the Body because the ultimate effect of functioning in these ways is a gift or giving to the whole Church. When each believer functions and does his business, the result is giving to the whole group. The word for gift in the Greek is *charisma*, which is related to the word for grace, *charis*. By grace, God pours out of His goodness and favor to make it possible for this giving to have an effect and to accomplish a purpose. So what are these "givings" to the Church and what are the effects?

The first block of four are: prophesying, ministering, teaching and comforting. We can see that these are general words that are describing the functioning of members in the Body. They are not the specific gift ministries of a prophet or teacher. We can understand these four functions by taking a brief look at the four major kinds of tissue: connective, muscle, blood, and epithelial.

Connective tissue is made up of fibroblast cells or connective cells. It forms the tissue in bones, cartilage, tendons and also supportive tissue for the inner organs. Its main functions are to connect, transfer and join. Muscle tissue was pictured earlier and described. It is the tissue that generates movement, support, doing and working, and its main job is service. Notice how this is lines up with the function listed in Romans 12. The blood is the vehicle of transmitting the red blood cells that carry oxygen to every part of the body. It is not always listed as tissue, but I believe it fits here because it is the communicating and circulating tissue of the body, just like teaching. Epithelial tissue is made up of epithelial cells that have joined together. They form the skin, the lining of all the organs, and the lining of the blood vessels. Their job is to cover, protect, renew, and strengthen. This is parallel to the comforter of Romans 12:7.

EXAMPLES OF FUNCTIONS

I have prepared a chart that outlines the functions, their meaning and comparison to the types of tissue. Then I have searched in the New Testament for people who exemplify these functions with the scripture references. We will look at the first four functions of the members in the order of their appearance in Romans 12.

FUNCTION	MEANING	TYPE OF CELL	EXAMPLE	VERSES
Prophesying	Connecting, transferring, building, cohering or joining	Connective	Judas & Silas Philip's daughters	Acts15:31,32 Acts 21:9
Ministering	Doing, attending, working, serving	Muscle	John Mark Timothy & Erastus Onesimus	Acts 13:5 Acts 19:22 Philemon 10-16
Teaching	Developing, growing, circulating, imparting	Blood	Apollos Priscilla & Aquila Zenas	Acts 18:24-28 I Cor. 16:19 Titus 3:13
Comforting	Covering, protecting, strengthening, encouraging, consoling	Epithelial	Philemon Phoebe	Philemon Romans 16:1

1) Prophesying

Regarding prophecy, "in the New Testament, as in the Old, the prominent idea is not *prediction,* but the inspired delivery of warning, exhortations, instruction, judging, and making manifest the secrets of the heart."[11] When one prophesies, he is building a connection between God and man by bringing inspired words from God. These words also build connections between people. Some synonyms for prophesying here in more general terms would be connecting, transferring, building, cohering or joining.

Acts 15:32 (MGI):
And with an abundance of the word Judas and Silas strengthened the brothers and established those of the household, because they also were prophets.

After the Jerusalem Council where the issue was discussed whether the Gentiles needed to be circumcised and convert to Judaism, Judas and Silas were sent to Antioch to report back to the Church. They are called prophets here, so were especially adept at this kind of exhortation. But in Romans 12, the function of prophesying is a general term and any believer can prophesy. Prophecy is building up, exhorting and comforting.

I Corinthians 14:3, 4:
But he that prophesieth speaketh unto men to edification, and exhortation, and comfort.
He that speaketh in an <u>unknown</u> tongue edifieth himself; but he that prophesieth edifieth the church.

---

[11] Vincent, Marvin R. *Word Studies in the New Testament,* p. 156.

Philip was one of the original seven deacons appointed in Acts chapter 6 who did evangelistic work and then settled in Caesarea. He had four "unmarried daughters" who prophesied. The time this verse occurs is when Paul and his friends are on the way to Jerusalem and must have been very encouraging for them.

Acts 21:9:
And the same man had four daughters, virgins, which did prophesy.

2) Ministering

Ministering simply means serving. It can be of any kind of service, but there is always the effect of movement, doing, attending, or work. Ministering is any kind of work that meets needs. On their first missionary journey, Paul and Barnabas took John Mark with them and John Mark served and took care of them.

Acts 13:5:
And when they were at Salamis, they preached the word of God in the synagogues of the Jews: and they had also John to their minister.

Timothy and Erastus accompanied Paul on his third missionary journey and were instrumental in taking care of the people in various cities when Paul moved on.

Acts 19:22:
So he sent into Macedonia two of them that ministered unto him, Timotheus and Erastus; but he himself stayed in Asia for a season.

Onesimus is a very vivid example of a minister. He was a runaway slave belonging to a man named Philemon and had lived in Colossae. He had run away to Rome, where he met Paul and had become a Christian. The letter to Philemon is a request from Paul to Philemon that Onesimus be received back in Colossae as a brother because of his service to Paul.

Philemon 10-16:
I beseech thee for my son Onesimus, whom I have begotten in my bonds:
Which in time past was to thee unprofitable, but now profitable to thee and to me:
Whom I have sent again: thou therefore receive him, that is, mine own bowels:
Whom I would have retained with me, that in thy stead he might have ministered unto me in the bonds of the gospel:
But without thy mind would I do nothing; that thy benefit should not be as it were of necessity, but willingly.
For perhaps he therefore departed for a season, that thou shouldest receive him for ever;
Not now as a servant, but above a servant, a brother beloved, specially to me, but how much more unto thee, both in the flesh, and in the Lord?

3) Teaching

Teaching has several synonyms: developing, growing, circulating, imparting, and communicating. The basic key to teaching is first to be a learner. The teacher gives what he has learned so others can learn and understand. Apollos is called an eloquent and diligent teacher.

Acts 18:24-28:
And a certain Jew named Apollos, born at Alexandria, an eloquent
man, and mighty in the scriptures, came to Ephesus.
This man was instructed in the way of the Lord; and being fervent
in the spirit, he spake and taught diligently the things of the Lord,
knowing only the baptism of John.
And he began to speak boldly in the synagogue: whom when
Aquila and Priscilla had heard, they took him unto them, and
expounded unto him the way of God more perfectly.
And when he was disposed to pass into Achaia, the brethren wrote,
exhorting the disciples to receive him: who, when he was come,
helped them much which had believed through grace:
For he mightily convinced the Jews, and that publickly, shewing by
the scriptures that Jesus was Christ.

When Aquila and Priscilla heard his teaching, they took him aside and explained about being born again and who Jesus the Messiah was. They were teaching Apollos, who in turn taught others.

Zenas is called a "lawyer" in the King James Version, but this word really means scribe. The scribes were skilled in writing and understanding the law and known as the teachers of the time of the first century.

Titus 3:13:
Bring Zenas the lawyer and Apollos on their journey diligently,
that nothing be wanting unto them.

4) Comforting

Comforting can also be translated helping, aiding, or assisting. Other synonyms would be covering, protecting,

31

renewing, strengthening, and consoling. There are many ways to comfort one another, by a touch, a word, an action. Anything that encourages and aids a person is comfort. Love is the biggest thing that truly consoles and helps someone. Philemon refreshed the saints with his love.

> *Philemon 4-7:*
> *I thank my God, making mention of thee always in my prayers,*
> *Hearing of thy love and faith, which thou hast toward the Lord Jesus, and toward all saints;*
> *That the communication of thy faith may become effectual by the acknowledging of every good thing which is in you in Christ Jesus.*
> *For we have great joy and consolation in thy love, because the bowels of the saints are refreshed by thee, brother.*

The last three "gifts" in Romans 12 are giving, leading and being merciful. Giving means to bestow, confer, or yield. It is to be done with simplicity, which is also often translated liberally or generously. Leading is a general term and does not refer to a particular office in the Church. In order to lead, one must do it with diligence, haste and care. The act of leading is not a haphazard task. Peter Wagner describes this gift as "the special ability…to set goals in accordance with God's purpose for the future and to communicate these goals to others in such a way that they voluntarily and harmoniously work together to accomplish those goals for the glory of God."[12] Being merciful is to have kindness or good will towards the miserable and the afflicted, joined with a desire to help them.

These last three kinds of functions of giving, leading and being merciful line up with three other kinds of tissue. These are

---

[12] Wagner, C. Peter. *Finding Your Spiritual Gifts*, p. 9.

fat tissue, nerve tissue and glandular tissue. Fat cells, as we saw in the previous chapter, are very important to the body. They store nutrients and are continually giving out and bestowing good things that the body needs.

Nerve cells join forces to form the brain tissue and spinal cord, and are also very important in the functioning of the body. Their function is to stimulate, guide and direct, just as leaders of any kind do. There are very specialized kinds of nerves and someone who has a medical or scientific background could probably do a study of this one area alone and find many comparisons.

Gland cells are also very varied, but one of the most important things they do is form the lymphatic tissue. The whole lymphatic system is designed to care for, to heal, and to help the body. I found a description of a gland in Gray's Anatomy that would also portray the function of someone who is merciful: "the essential parts, therefore, of a secreting gland are *cells*, which have the power of extracting from the blood certain matters, and in some cases converting them into new chemical compounds...."[13] A person who is merciful helps to change a potentially negative situation into a positive one by their love and care. White cells also belong in this class and are part of the lymphatic system. We will be studying more about them in a future chapter. Let us see examples of these last three functions.

---

[13] Gray, Henry, *Anatomy, Descriptive and Surgical*, a Revised American. From the Fifteenth English Edition., p. 1146.

FUNCTION	MEANING	TYPE OF CELL	EXAMPLE	VERSES
Giving (with generosity)	Bestowing, conferring, yielding, giving	Fat	Lydia Mary	Acts 16:13-15 Romans 16:6
Leading (with diligence)	Leading, guiding, stimulating	Nerve	Ananias	Acts 9:10-17
Being merciful (with cheerfulness)	Caring, healing, soothing, delivering	Gland	Dorcas Jesus (Justus) Epaphras	Acts 9:36 Col. 4:11 Col. 4:12

5) Giving

Lydia is an example of a woman who opened her home with great hospitality to Paul when he first came to Philippi. She did it with generosity and simplicity.

Acts 16:13-15:
And on the sabbath we went out of the city by a river side, where prayer was wont to be made; and we sat down, and spake unto the women which resorted thither.
And a certain woman named Lydia, a seller of purple, of the city of Thyatira, which worshipped God, heard us: whose heart the Lord opened, that she attended unto the things which were spoken of Paul.
And when she was baptized, and her household, she besought us, saying, If ye have judged me to be faithful to the Lord, come into my house, and abide there. And she constrained us.

There is also a little known woman named Mary who toiled and labored for the believers who lived in Rome.

Romans 16:6:
Greet Mary, who bestowed much labour on us.

6) Leading

Ananias is the "certain disciple" who came and ministered to Saul after his conversion on the road to Damascus. He was not afraid to follow the word of the Lord to him and later introduced Saul to the disciples.

Acts 9:10-17:
And there was a certain disciple at Damascus, named Ananias; and to him said the Lord in a vision, Ananias. And he said, Behold, I am here, Lord.
And the Lord said unto him, Arise, and go into the street which is called Straight, and inquire in the house of Judas for one called Saul, of Tarsus; for, behold, he prayeth,
And Ananias went his way, and entered into the house; and putting his hands on him said, Brother Saul, the Lord, even Jesus, that appeared unto thee in the way as thou camest, hath sent me, that thou mightest receive thy sight, and be filled with the Holy Ghost.

Ananias is not mentioned at any other time in Acts, but he probably continued to minister and lead the believers in Damascus.

7) Being merciful

Acts 9:36:
Now there was at Joppa a certain disciple named Tabitha, which by interpretation is called Dorcas: this woman was full of good works and almsdeeds which she did.

The people in Joppa loved Dorcas and were very upset when she died. Peter came to raise her from the dead and the testimony about her is that she did many acts of charity.

Being merciful requires service that is not necessarily easy or pleasant to do because the people receiving mercy do not always deserve it. Many times it requires much prayer on people's behalf. Mr. Wagner describes mercy as "the special ability ...to feel genuine empathy and compassion for individuals (both Christian and non-Christian) who suffer distressing physical, mental or emotional problems, and to translate that compassion into cheerfully done deeds which reflect Christ's love and alleviate the suffering."[14] What a beautiful way to express the functioning of one who is being merciful!

Justus and Epaphras traveled and worked with Paul, but their hearts were with the people of Colossae.

> *Colossians 4:11, 12:*
> *And Jesus, which is called Justus, who are of the circumcision. These only are my fellowworkers unto the kingdom of God, which have been a comfort unto me.*
> *Epaphras, who is one of you, a servant of Christ, saluteth you, always labouring fervently for you in prayers, that ye may stand perfect and complete in all the will of God.*

Epaphras demonstrated his compassion for the people by praying for them fervently.

As you can see from these passages and the description of the seven functions, they were performed by many kinds of

---

[14] Wagner, C. Peter. *Finding Your Spiritual Gifts.*, p. 9.

believers. If there had been more room in Acts, perhaps we would find many more incidents that would describe these "givings" to the Church. But what would be more fun is to view the members in your Church or fellowship and see the different functions in **our** book of Acts!

We started out this chapter by asking the question of why do schisms happen so often and what we can do about it. We can now see that one reason for these things is misunderstanding about the different "businesses" that believers have. We have seen that there is much variety in using the general terms of prophesying, ministering, teaching, comforting, giving, leading, and being merciful. These are broad terms and describe many aspects of work that believers have to do. If we understand more about the kinds of work of others who are not necessarily exactly the same as us, we will have less and less division. We can encourage one another to get busy prophesying, ministering, teaching, giving, comforting, leading, and being merciful, for these will allow the grace of God to be poured out in application in our lives.

One of the key things that we must continue to remember is that this comparison of the physical body is an analogy and as with all analogies it will break down at some point. When we are talking about individuals and their functions, people have long suits in particular areas, but that does not mean that they cannot do several or even all of the different functions described in Romans 12. Even in a study of the types of cells, there are many specialty cells and varieties of each kind, but normally they do not overlap in their functions as people can do.

Chapter 4

LOVE IS THE GLUE

I explained in the introduction that this book has snapshots of the physical body so that we may understand more about the spiritual Body of Christ. In this chapter we are going to look at ligaments, which are a kind of connective tissue, and see how they compare to the Body of Christ. Connective tissue functions similarly to glue because both serve to connect things together. There are different kinds and brands of glue: wood, rubber cement, Elmer's, Super Glue, etc. You choose the right glue depending on the material you want to stick together. For the Body of Christ to stick together, God has given us his love to serve as the glue or connecting element.

In Colossians, God specifically defines love as a bond. Here are a few translations of Colossians 3:14.

> *KJV: And above all these things put on charity, which is the bond of perfectness.*
> *ESV And above all these put on love, which binds together everything together in perfect harmony.*
> *NASB Put on love, which is the perfect bond of unity.*

A definition of the Greek word for bond is "the ligaments by which the members of the human body are united together."[15] God calls love the ligaments in the Body of Christ and the ligaments help to hold all the bones together.

Perfectness means maturity in Aramaic. Love is the uniting bond of maturity. As we put on the love of God we will grow up

---

[15] Thayer, Joseph. *The New Thayer's Greek-English Lexicon*, p. 601.

in Christ (Ephesians 4:15), be bonded together and begin to work as a unit.

There are two things that make the Body of Christ work together. We have a common connecting point and we are knit together in love. The connecting points in a physical body are the joints. A joint is where two bones come together and is the point where the bones touch. Wherever two bones are joined, elastic, fibrous tissue called ligaments are present to tie the bones together. Without being tied together, the bones could not function or move. It is the same picture with the Body of Christ.

Everyone who is born-again is given the gift of Christ. Our connecting point is that we all have the same gift and the same measure of Holy Spirit. We are all bonded together by the gift of Holy Spirit, no matter where we are or how different we may be. No person has any more Spirit than another because we have the measure of the fullness of Christ, which is complete.

Ephesians 4:7:
But unto every one of us is given grace according to the measure of the gift of Christ.

We have the same measure of the Spirit that was in Christ. That means we can walk like he walked, with his love, with his compassion, with his peace and with the same confidence that he had as God's Son. Think about how he manifested love and compassion toward the people he was ministering to and with and know that you have that same gift!

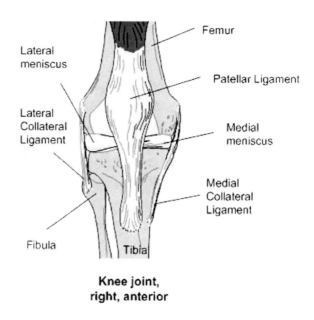

**Knee joint,
right, anterior**

As you can see from the above illustration of the cross section of a knee, without binding ligaments, the body would fall apart and we would be a pile of unmoving bones. The ligaments connect the bones together around a joint and are the connecting tissue in between groups of bones. They protect the bones from rubbing on each other and they cushion the impact of movement in the physical body.

When love is present, it ties everything in the Body of Christ together and nourishment is ministered. Exactly how this works is explained in Colossians.

Colossians 2:19:
And not holding the Head, from which all the body by joints and bands having nourishment ministered, and knit together, increaseth with the increase of God.

Starting from the head (Christ) downward, nourishment is ministered and we are knit together by joints and bands. As I explained, the joint is the Spirit and the bands are love. If we have the gift of Holy Spirit, but not the love of God being manifested, the Body lacks the nourishment it needs to accomplish anything for God.

The word for "knit together" is also used in two other places in Ephesians and Colossians.

Ephesians 4:16 (MGI):
And from him the whole body is fit together and is knit together in all the joints, according to the gift that is given by measure to each member for the growth of the body, that its building up would be accomplished in love.

Knit together can be translated "molded" or "woven together." Ligaments are not just lined up side by side, they are woven together. This set-up allows for flexibility. The words for knit together in the King James Version are translated "compacted" and also describes the fact that we are to be intertwined. It is the responsibility of every believer to walk and to be energized by the Spirit so that at their joint, the point of contact, they can supply that which is needed to the Body of Christ. If we don't individually walk by the Spirit, we rob the Body of what we are supposed to be giving to it. Also we have to walk in love in order for the Body to be built up. We can have all kinds of signs, miracles, and wonders but without love, we are nothing. (I Corinthians 13:1-3).

Love is what causes growth and promotes health. When we are knit together in love it is an acknowledgement of the mystery.

Love produces comfort and testifies that we are all part of the Body of Christ and sons and daughters of God.

Colossians 2:2:
That their hearts might be comforted, being knit together in love, and unto all riches of the full assurance of understanding, to the acknowledgement of the mystery of God, and of the Father, and of Christ;

The mystery of the Body of Christ is also illustrated as the Church being a family. We have God as our Father and each other as brothers and sisters in Christ. Just as an earthly family is tied together by love and develops relationships, we are a spiritual family and need to be tied together by love. Our family of God extends over the entire world and we need to recognize the vastness of this reality. There are numerous accounts where God refers to us as his children and we are called brothers and sisters in Christ. Start to think about how close a family which is joined by blood can be in strength, love, compassion, closeness and care. Then you can begin to see God's vision of how powerful the family of God can be when we are joined by Spirit and the bond of perfect love.

To better understand what it means to walk in love, let us consider how God and his son Jesus Christ exemplify the characteristics of love.

Ephesians 5:1, 2:
Be ye therefore followers of God, as dear children;
And walk in love, as Christ also hath loved us, and hath given himself for us an offering and a sacrifice to God for a sweetsmelling savour.

Love always has an element of giving. Jesus Christ made known the true nature of God. He always did the Father's will. His example of walking in love was to willingly lay down his life as the perfect sacrifice.

Because of love, God gave his Son on our behalf so that we would not have to die, but would have everlasting life!

John 3:16:
For God so loved the world, that he gave his only begotten son that whosoever believeth in him should not perish, but have everlasting life.

Being knit together in love and allowing love to bind us together like the ligaments do is a life of giving and service to one another. When we do this together, then the bond will be very strong. The supply of the Spirit will be energized in each believer and the Body will move together.

Chapter 5

INTERCESSION AND THE BODY OF CHRIST

At the end of the description of putting on the armor of God in Ephesians 6 is a key verse about prayer. The verb in English is "praying" and shows that there is a continuation of "putting on" the armor in its various parts. In the *Aramaic Peshitta New Testament Translation*, verse 18 begins with "and" to show the continuation of action needed.

Ephesians 6:18 (MGI):
And with all prayers and with all petitions, pray at all times spiritually, and in prayer, be watchful in every season, praying continually and interceding for all the holy [ones],

The person who has put on the armor is now exhorted to continue by praying at all times in the spirit and making intercession. The first exhortation before the intercession is to be watchful. You put on the armor of God and then continue to pray and watch. As you watch, God shows you the places where the enemy is trying to attack, first in your life and then in the lives of other believers. As you pray, God gives you the knowledge and wisdom (revelation) needed to implement your "equipment" in order to defeat the enemy. That is how the armor works. The armor itself is all that Jesus Christ is in you, by way of the Spirit. What you do is use the armor to defeat the attacks of the enemy.

Here is how the intercession comes in. You make supplication on behalf of all the saints. What this kind of prayer does is petitions God to energize the Spirit on behalf of others. It asks for the wisdom of how to utilize the sword and shield in the best fashion. If you ask that for others, then when others are attacked, you can help them. In an attack, many times the man next to you has a different view and he can see the enemy sneaking up on you from the side and shout, "Watch on the right!" That is intercession.

The word intercession comes from two Latin words, meaning to move between. I put my sword (revelation) up to move in between you and the enemy to help in the battle. This is why we need intercession. I believe that when a person is interceding they are like the white cells in the lymphatic system of the body.

The purpose of white cells is to protect the body, to fight off infection and attack from outside sources, and to help the body to heal. If you get stung by a bee, for example, the brain notifies the white cells that they need to marshal together and go to the area. First, certain kinds of white cells surround the foreign particle and form a shield around it so that it doesn't affect the rest of the body. Then, they multiply and work hard to force the body to reject the foreign substance. White cells attack the poison and remnants of the stinger. Eventually, if there are enough white cells and they are allowed to work, the wound closes and the body heals itself from there.

We can easily see the comparison in the spiritual realm. Believers are made aware (either by revelation or by otherwise being informed) of a need and go to surround the area of hurt in the Body with their prayers. They are supposed to continue praying until the foreign substance is removed and the Body is healed in that area.

Let's see this application by looking at a few different kinds of white cells. It is so marvelous to see the way God has designed the physical body to cover every possibility and also to see what a perfect illustration it is for the way he designed the Body of Christ to work! One kind of white cell is called a macrophagocyte. It is a very large cell and is sometimes also called a "scavenger cell." It goes around and actually swallows up dirt, bacteria, or any harmful substance. Has there been a time in your life when you prayed for someone else's horrible situation and it was relieved? You were behaving like a macrophagocyte. Below is a picture of a macrophage eliminating something from the bloodstream.

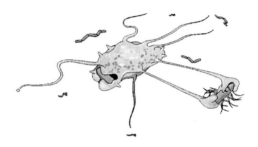

Another kind of white cell is a lymphocyte, sometimes called a "killer T-cell." Antibodies can attach to the surface of these cells that search out harmful viruses. The antibodies are released from the white cell and capture the harmful viruses, making them harmless so that they can be eaten by other white cells. The lymphocyte actually "remembers" the exact shape of the antibody needed, and as it divides, the body can then produce large numbers of free-moving antibodies useful against the same disease. This is the why inoculation works for diseases such as smallpox, measles, etc. The body has produced a large quantity of antibodies to combat those particular viruses. There are about 100,000 receptors on the lymphocyte's cellular membrane that enable the cell to recognize one specific foreign substance.

In addition to the fact that white cells can move in and out of the walls of the blood vessels to do their work in any part of the body, there is a whole network of lymph nodes throughout the body, approximately 1,000 to 1,500 of them. These nodes act as filtering stations for harmful substances that come into the body through various routes.

The following is an illustration of the lymph nodes in the body.

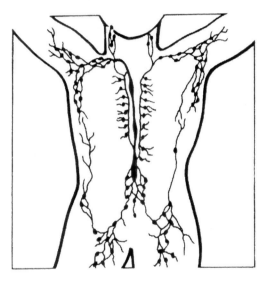

See how they are strategically stationed throughout the center of the body. Today in the Church we can see this kind of network and to see "nodes" forming where believers pray together on a continual basis. They are carrying out the exact function of lymph nodes except in the whole Body of Christ both locally and globally.

There is one more kind of white cell that is fascinating. It is called a B cell because it is produced in the bone marrow. B cells eliminate antigens or foreign substances by releasing kinds of blood proteins called immunoglobulins. These products are soluble so they actually dissolve the foreign substance. With the aid of another kind of T cell called the helper T cell, they can also transform into a larger cell called a blast cell. The blast cell begins to divide rapidly, forming a clone of identical cells.

Some of these blast cells transform further into plasma cells, in essence, antibody-producing factories. These plasma cells can produce a single type of antibody at a rate of about 2,000 antibodies per second! Some B cells do not transform into plasma cells but serve as "memory cells." They closely resemble the original B cell but have a memory of the invasion of that antigen, and so can respond more quickly to a second invasion.

Believers can act as the various kinds of white cells and perform specific immune system functions, so that harmful viruses and bacteria are destroyed and they cannot hurt the Body. White cells spend about 30 minutes a day in the lymph nodes and re-circulate about 50 times per day between the blood and lymph tissues. There are approximately 1 trillion T cells and 1 trillion B cells plus about 10 billion antigen-specific cells in the lymph tissue and the blood. We need white cells!!!

We have seen that individuals are like the various kinds of cells and that cells bond together to form tissue. In this brief explanation of white cells, we have also seen that there is a tremendous variety of sizes and shapes and specific functions. This illustrates that even within a certain type of function such as being merciful with intercession, there is tremendous variety. The cells work together in many different ways. So it is important to remember that each person functions in his own unique way and the daily challenge is to work together to perform similar jobs and to endeavor to understand how to complement each other. We need every kind and type and no function is unnecessary!

Chapter 6

STAND IN TRUE GRACE

The framework of the physical body is the skeletal system, or structure of bones. This system is closely tied in to the muscular system. Muscles attached to the firm surfaces of your bones enable you to move. Sometimes these two systems are called the muscular-skeleton system or locomotor system because they are so closely aligned. The skeletal muscles make up more than 40 percent of the weight of a man, slightly less for a woman.[16] For many of us, the word "muscle" calls up an image of a professional body-builder or trainer with bulging muscle mass. But everyone has over 500 voluntary muscles to use as the "machines" of the body. [17]

Muscles are anchored firmly to the bones by tendons and ligaments. We have already seen in the chapter on "Love is the Glue" that the ligaments are the love of God. I believe that the framework, or bone structure, that provides form and stability in the Church is truth and the movement of the service of ministering in the Body happens when believers operate the manifestations of the Spirit, energized by grace. We can see in the following diagram how integrally these three elements are intertwined when we look at how the muscles are attached to the bones with the tendons.

---

[16] Bruun, Ruth Dowling, *The Human Body*, p. 39.
[17] Marieb, Elaine N. *Essentials of Human Anatomy & Physiology*, p. 139.

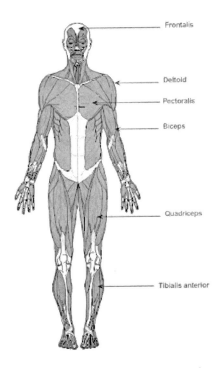

Grace and truth both came by Jesus, the Messiah. In other words, the understanding of what grace and truth were came when the fullness of the understanding of who Jesus Christ is was made manifest.

I Corinthians 1:4:
I thank my God always on your behalf, for the grace of God which is given you by Jesus Christ;

John 1:16-18:
And of his fulness have all we received, and grace for grace.
For the law was given by Moses, but grace and truth came by Jesus Christ.

No man hath seen God at any time; the only begotten Son, which is in the bosom of the Father, he hath declared him.

The phrase "grace and truth" is a figure of speech, *hendiadys*, that is two nouns said, but one thing meant. The two nouns can be put together and said as "true grace" or "grace-filled truth." They mean more than the individual words mean by themselves.[18] Usually the concept is so big, it needs to have this emphasis in order to communicate how all-encompassing true grace is. Just as the skeletal and muscular systems work together so integrally, so do grace and truth.

Truth is one of those words that is very difficult to define. Often, truth is defined as being the word of God. But I believe in this context of the first chapter of John, truth should be rendered more accurately as truthfulness.

John 1:14 (MGI):
And the word became flesh and lived among us and we saw his glory, the glory as of the unique one who was from the Father, who is full of grace and truthfulness.

The unique nature of Jesus as the firstborn son of God is what is communicated by "truthfulness." His standing, his relationship with God as his Father and his nature of righteousness before God is summed up here in John as "truth." We have been given all of the same qualities and sonship rights as Jesus had. This is our framework and the basis or foundation of our lives.

In Ephesians it is described as a "new man."

---

[18] Bullinger, E.W. *Figures of Speech Used in the Bible*, p. 663.

Ephesians 4:24:
And that ye put on the new man, which after God is created in
righteousness and true holiness.

Without the bone structure, we could not stand. So in the Body of
Christ, we stand in the righteousness and truth of who we are in
Christ. That becomes the framework whereby we can move and
function. Then grace is like the muscles in the locomotor system.
All the work of the Spirit is energized by God through grace.

The manifestations of the Spirit are the evidence of God's
grace being poured out in specific ways. These manifestations are
listed in I Corinthians 12.

I Corinthians 12:6-10:
And there are diversities of operations, but it is the same God
which worketh all in all.
But the manifestation of the Spirit is given to every man to profit
withal.
For to one is given by the Spirit the word of wisdom; to another the
word of knowledge by the same Spirit;
To another faith by the same Spirit; to another the gifts of healing
by the same Spirit;
To another the working of miracles; to another prophecy; to another
discerning of spirits; to another divers kinds of tongues; to another
the interpretation of tongues:

There are nine different ways that the Spirit comes into evidence
and just as muscles work together, so do these individual
manifestations.

The framework is truth, like the bones which support the body and give it its shape and form and then grace is the cause of movement, like the muscles. We first need to look at the definition of grace and then see the verses where these two concepts are tied together in Acts and the epistles.

Grace has often been translated "divine favor." This does not show the complete picture of the meaning of the word in either Greek or Aramaic. *Charis* in Greek comes from the same root as *chairo*, to rejoice, and primarily means, "that which gives joy or pleasure and hence outward beauty and loveliness." The idea of rejoicing is inherent then in the concept of grace. The specific definition of grace is: "*based on the emphasis of* freeness *in the gift or favor, and, as commonly in New Testament, denoting the free, spontaneous, absolute loving-kindness of God toward men....*"[19] In Aramaic, the root word for grace means "to be good" and the word for goodness is a related noun to grace. So if we put the Greek and Aramaic definitions together, I would summarize the definition of grace as **God's goodness and love that causes rejoicing.**

It is the Spirit energizing that gift of grace within us that causes the Body to function and to have the ministries come into fruition, so to speak. Paul refers to his life as a minister as "according to the grace of God" and he exhorts Timothy to be strong in grace.

Ephesians 3:7:
Whereof I was made a minister, according to the gift of the grace of God given unto me by the effectual working of his power.

---

[19] Vincent, Marvin, *Word Studies in the New Testament*, p. 259.

II Timothy 2:1:
Thou therefore, my son, be strong in the grace that is in Christ Jesus.

Now we can begin to see how grace is an integral part of the operation of the Spirit and how they work together. After the day of Pentecost, there were many people being born again. Signs, miracles and wonders were abounding. In Acts 3, the man at the temple gate Beautiful was healed. And this is the testimony about the ongoing results of that healing.

Acts 4:33:
And with great power gave the apostles witness of the resurrection of the Lord Jesus: and great grace was upon them all.

In Antioch, when the Gentiles first started believing, Barnabas went to Antioch and "saw" great grace.

Acts 11:23:
Who, when he came, and had seen the grace of God, was glad, and exhorted them all, that with purpose of heart they would cleave unto the Lord.

What did Barnabas see? He saw that the Gentile believers had spoken in tongues and were manifesting the power of God exactly as had happened to the believers in Judea! When Paul and Barnabas were on their first missionary journey in Antioch of Pisidia, they exhorted the believers to be "followers of the grace of God."

Acts 13:43 (MGI):
And after the synagogue was dismissed, many Judeans followed them and also proselytes who feared God. And they were speaking and persuading them to be follower[s] of the grace of God.

Later on in Iconium, Paul and Barnabas were speaking boldly and many signs and wonders bore witness to the grace of God.

Acts 14:3:
Long time therefore abode they speaking boldly in the Lord, which gave testimony unto the word of his grace, and granted signs and wonders to be done by their hands.

The miracles were the visible witness of God's goodness being poured out to the people. We can certainly see that when these things happened, people were rejoicing!

To reign in life, we must come boldly to the throne of grace to find help in times of trial.

Hebrews 4:16:
Let us therefore come boldly unto the throne of grace, that we may obtain mercy, and find grace to help in time of need.

We cannot walk and function without grace. And as we move in this grace, the Body as a whole will find more grace being poured out to cause it to be strengthened and to stand.

In conclusion, we need to hold fast to the truth in Christ Jesus so that we can serve God. We then walk in grace and can please God.

Hebrews 12:28 (MGI):
Therefore, because we have received a kingdom that is unshakable,
we should hold fast to the grace, by which we may serve and may
please God, with reverence and with fear.

This takes walking by the Spirit and "growing in grace."

II Peter 3:18:
But grow in grace, and in the knowledge of our Lord and Saviour
Jesus Christ. To him be glory both now and for ever. Amen.

As the physical body is able to stand and move when the bones, muscles and ligaments are working together, so the Body of Christ will be able to live and accomplish its designed purposes as we work together and stand in true grace.

Chapter 7

BODY SYSTEMS

Until this point in the book, we have been discussing the individual and his functions in the Body of Christ. Each person has the fullness of Christ in him and has a place to serve and function. But what about what are normally called the "gift ministries" of apostle, prophet, evangelist, pastor and teacher? Are these ministries something given by God in addition to the Holy Spirit within? Why are they called gifts? These are some of the questions that will be answered in the next two chapters.

I began to write this book originally because I was searching to understand what ministries are and how to explain their functions simply. Because my father was a chest surgeon, I have always been interested in the body and how it works. So God showed me a picture of how the ministries in the Church compare to the organs in the systems of the body. That set me on a quest over a number of years to study the subject from the Bible. I believe that the comparison will help us to understand what the gift ministries are and that there is tremendous diversity in their operation.

Ministers in the Body of Christ operate like the organs in five different systems of the body. Apostles are related to the nervous system, prophets to the respiratory system, evangelists to the reproductive system, pastors to the digestive system and teachers to the circulatory system. The diversity of the organs and parts of these systems show that there is a wide range of purposes in the operation of these ministries.

Before we explore the comparisons of the organs of the body with the gift ministries, it is necessary to explain what the ministries are and how they function. I am using the term "gift ministries" and "ministries" to mean the people who serve in the Body in these five ways. The key passage regarding the ministries is in Ephesians 4:7-13.

Ephesians 4:7:
But unto every one of us is given grace according to the measure of the gift of Christ.

Everyone who is born again of God's Spirit is given grace in the measure of the gift of Christ. This is the fullness of all that the Messiah was and is and it is **in** us. It certainly is God's goodness and mercy that would allow us to have this gift! The word for Messiah comes from a root word in Aramaic that has two meanings, to anoint and to measure. Normally Christ is translated the "anointed one", but it could also be translated "the full measure." We have Christ in us (Colossians 1:27) and thus we have the full measure of the Spirit that was given to Jesus, the Messiah.

Ephesians 4:8-10:
Wherefore he saith, When he ascended up on high, he led captivity captive, and gave gifts unto men.
(Now that he ascended, what is it but that he also descended first into the lower parts of the earth?
He that descended is the same also that ascended up far above all heavens, that he might fill all things.)

Now Ephesians 4 goes on to explain what happened after the ascension of Christ. He ascended up "on high" and verse 10 further clarifies where that is and says, "far above all heavens."

This word for heavens is the Greek word *ouranos* and means, "the region above the sidereal heavens, the seat of order of things eternal and consummately perfect where God dwells and other heavenly beings."[20] The sidereal heavens means all the stars. Christ ascended above the stars to where the throne of God is. What happened when he was there?

Ephesians 4:8 shows us what Christ did after the ascension. *He led captivity captive and gave gifts to men.* In Aramaic, the phrase "led captivity captive" could be literally translated, "he captured captivity" or "he captured what is captive." Who was in captivity at this time? All of mankind! They were held captive in the web of the Evil one and his control over us. Because of what Christ accomplished in his death and resurrection, this control has been broken. Everyone who accepts Jesus as Lord and believes that God raised him from the dead can be **saved** – rescued, no longer captive!

Ephesians 4:11:
And he gave some, apostles; and some, prophets; and some, evangelists; and some, pastors and teachers;

The second part of what Christ did after he led captivity captive was to give gifts to men and Ephesians explains that these gifts are apostles, prophets, evangelists, pastors and teachers. Some Christians refer to these ministries as "ascension gifts" and this helps to clarify when they were given. In order to understand this phrase about giving gifts to men, we need to look at the passage in the Old Testament from where this is quoted.

---

[20] *The New Thayer's Greek-English Lexicon of the New Testament*, p. 465.

Psalm 68:18:
Thou hast ascended on high, thou hast led captivity captive: thou
hast received gifts for men; yea, for the rebellious also, that the
LORD God might dwell among them.

The phrase "for men" in Hebrew may be translated "consisting of men" or "among men." Christ received gifts to distribute among men. What were those gifts? God calls them apostles, prophets, etc. Those men who have this office are themselves the gifts! Their whole life is the gift to the Body of Christ. The purpose for these gifts is clear from Psalm 68: "that the Lord God may dwell among them." All of the gift ministries have the same purpose–to help to facilitate and understand the dwelling place of God among men.

The Layman's Handy Commentary on the Bible puts it succinctly: "They who are ministers of His gifts are themselves gifts from Him to the Church."[21] The key idea here is that there is not some special gift that is above the "fullness of Christ" that everyone has, but what constitutes an apostle or prophet or any other minister is that their whole lives are the gift to the Church so that they may function as Christ did in all of these ministries. Christ himself was all five types of the ministers and it is clear that his whole life was a gift. Now he has distributed this same authority and these men and women as gifts to give their lives to the Church.

The concept of what these gifts are is further clarified in the understanding that this passage from Psalms was referring to a triumphal procession. The Romans in the first century were also

---

[21] Ellicott, Charles, ed. *The Layman's Handy Commentary on the Bible*, p. 186.

very familiar with the processions of the returning conqueror who would lead his captives and display them. There was a custom in such triumphs of distributing presents among the soldiers and the crowds. The Greek word *doma*, used here describing these gifts, has the connotation of the presents given by the conquering hero.

Doma is also used of a gift, as in a medicinal dose. It is a gift that provides something. What these gifts of men provide to the Church is explained in Ephesians 4.

Ephesians 4:12, 13:
For the perfecting of the saints, for the work of the ministry, for the edifying of the body of Christ:
Till we all come in the unity of the faith, and of the knowledge of the Son of God, unto a perfect man, unto the measure of the stature of the fulness of Christ:

"Perfecting" here means to furnish or equip. The Aramaic Peshitta text explains that equipping as "maturing of the saints." The purpose of these people given to the Church is serve and to build up the Body of Christ. There may be various ways to describe what the gift ministries are, but it is clear that they are to help the believers to become more like Christ.

Now that we have set the background of the gift ministries, we need to look at the individual offices and the explanation of them from the New Testament. There are five offices: apostle, prophet, evangelist, pastor and teacher. Some would put the pastor and teacher together in one office because the Greek uses the word "some" only four times instead of five, but the Aramaic repeats the word "some" five times. Practically it can be seen that some people are pastors and some teachers and whereas there is some cross-over, there still is a distinction in the office.

What is an apostle? The simple meaning of the Greek word is "a sent one." It can be translated as a delegate, messenger, or representative. Apostles are sent to bring liberty in a certain area so the Body can move. Jesus Christ is listed as the first "messenger."

Hebrews 3:1-3:
Wherefore, holy brethren, partakers of the heavenly calling, consider the Apostle and High Priest of our profession, Christ Jesus;
Who was faithful to him that appointed him, as also Moses was faithful in all his house.
For this man was counted worthy of more glory than Moses, inasmuch as he who hath builded the house hath more honour than the house.

Jesus Christ built the house and was faithful. These are two key characteristics of an apostle.

Apostles have certain jurisdictions. In Greek the word *apostolos* is used of men who were naval officers responsible for a fleet of ships or as an emissary of an expedition sent with a specific objective. Peter was called the apostle to Israel (I Peter 1:1) and Paul was sent to be an apostle to the Gentiles (Romans 11:13).

Like the nerves in the nervous system that spring from the spinal cord, the apostles stimulate and motivate the various parts of the Body. Even the original apostles were sent to specific areas and in oral history we have the records of at least some of them:

Peter was in Babylon, John went to Asia Minor, especially Ephesus, Thomas to India, especially southern India (where there are still many Christians today), Andrew to Romania and the area of the Black Sea. Matthew (Levi) went to the area of the Caspian Sea and Thaddeus to Syria and Edessa. These are only a few of the places that we know of from oral traditions and the early Church fathers.

Now some teachers in the Body of Christ teach that we no longer have apostles. (If we no longer have apostles, then it is possible we no longer have teachers and they would be out of work!) Others laud themselves as apostles because of wanting to be "over" others as the most prominent and "best" ministry. This is cited from I Corinthians 12.

I Corinthians 12:28:
And God hath set some in the church, first apostles, secondarily prophets, thirdly teachers, after that miracles, then gifts of healings, helps, governments, diversities of tongues.

The emphasis in this verse is that **God** truly set the ministries and manifestations in the Church. It was his idea how the Body was to be set up. We need to remember that all ministries are **servants**. They serve the Body of Christ from underneath and uphold and build up the Body. We can see this from the nervous system. The nerves that stimulate the movement in one arm, for example, are not any better than the bronchial tubes that carry the oxygen to the body. They each have a specific purpose and none is more important than the other.

Prophets are like the respiratory system, which is also tied in to the lymphatic system. Both systems are responsible for providing the life-giving oxygen and for causing the nitrogen and other waste products to be removed from the body. The alveoli in the lungs are like small purifying filters. Here is a picture of the alveoli to illustrate this principle:

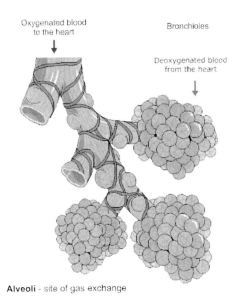

Oxygenated blood to the heart

Bronchioles

Deoxygenated blood from the heart

Alveoli - site of gas exchange

Comparing the Body of Christ with the human physical body is not meant to be exclusive in the sense that every type of cell and body part corresponds to the Body of Christ. However, there are certain patterns that can be seen in looking at the way the Church is supposed to function by understanding the physical body.

Prophecy is closely aligned with the idea of breath and the Spirit.

Psalm 33:6:
By the word of the LORD were the heavens made; and all the host of them by the breath of his mouth.

Prophets speak for God. We can see that speaking is tightly bound up with breath. Prophets have perception into the hearts of men and bring messages that are exhorting and also comforting. I think of it as "in with the good and out with the bad" as the physical body takes in oxygen and gets rid of nitrogen and other harmful substances. Prophets help believers sort things out.

Evangelists are aligned with the reproductive system, which is easy to see. These men and women are called to preach the gospel of the good news of Christ so that new believers may be added to the Body. However, they are also called to speak messages of encouragement to believers in the Body. This encouragement and undergirding acts like specific organs in the reproductive system, such as the uterus. The uterus is designed to cradle and support the developing baby.

> I Corinthians 1:23, 24:
> But we preach Christ crucified, unto the Jews a stumblingblock, and unto the Greeks foolishness;
> But unto them which are called, both Jews and Greeks, Christ the power of God, and the wisdom of God.

Evangelists preach Christ. Preaching is designed for those who are called, and also for the Church and those who are already saved.

> Colossians 1:27, 28:
> To whom God would make known what is the riches of the glory of this mystery among the Gentiles; which is Christ in you, the hope of glory:
> Whom we preach, warning every man, and teaching every man in all wisdom; that we may present every man perfect in Christ Jesus:

Pastors have the most variety in their functions. When compared to the digestive system, this is easy to see because of the variety of shapes and sizes of the digestive organs. The digestive system includes organs like the stomach, which is very acidic and churns up the food, as well as the intestines, which soothe and process the food sending necessary nutrients to all parts of the body. The following diagram of a portion of the digestive system will illustrate the variety of these organs.

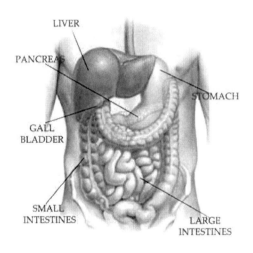

All of the organs of the digestive system have to do with feeding and providing nourishment to our physical body. The counsel of a pastor can pinpoint a person's problem and bring healing wholeness to his life.

Another illustration of pastors is that they are like shepherds taking care of a flock. This illustrations shows the same principle as the digestive system.

I Peter 5:2, 3:
Feed the flock of God which is among you, taking the oversight thereof, not by constraint, but willingly; not for filthy lucre, but of a ready mind; Neither as being lords over God's heritage, but being ensamples to the flock.

In Zechariah 11, we can see from the characteristics of a bad shepherd what the opposite would be.

Zechariah 11:16:
For, lo, I will raise up a shepherd in the land, which shall not visit those that be cut off, neither shall seek the young one, nor heal that that is broken, nor feed that that standeth still: but he shall eat the flesh of the fat, and tear their claws in pieces.

Pastors visit the sick and needy, take care of youth and elderly, provide healing and rest to the weary of heart and mind, gather and protect those in their care.

Last, but not least, teachers are like organs in the circulatory system. Their job and purpose is to bring understanding and to "circulate" the truth of the Word of God. Both the Hebrew and Aramaic words for "teach" mean to learn and to teach. A teacher is a learner first and then provides life-bringing understanding to others. This is remarkably how the entire blood system works. It takes in the things the body needs and sends those same things to the cells throughout the body. Jesus Christ was the master teacher, yet all he taught he learned from his heavenly Father.

Mark 6:2:
And when the sabbath day was come, he began to teach in the synagogue: and many hearing him were astonished, saying, From

whence hath this man these things? and what wisdom is this which is given unto him, that even such mighty works are wrought by his hands?

Paul was called a teacher as well as an apostle. At the end of his life, he was still teaching about the Lord Jesus Christ when he was in prison.

Acts 28:31:
Preaching the kingdom of God, and teaching those things which concern the Lord Jesus Christ, with all confidence, no man forbidding him.

In conclusion, these gift ministries or "ascension gifts" of apostle, prophet, evangelist, pastor and teacher are gifts to the Church. The whole life of the person is the gift to the Body of Christ. Their functions and purposes are consistently aligned with maturing, equipping and building up the Body of Christ. They promote Christ, they speak of Christ, they encourage people to walk like Christ, they exemplify the compassion of Christ and they teach of Christ.

Chapter 8

MINISTRIES IN THE EARLY CHURCH

We have learned that the ministries of apostles, prophets, evangelists, pastors and teachers are an outpouring of grace where the whole person's life becomes a gift to the Body of Christ. The gift is the person and they serve to accomplish God's purposes that are specific for the time and place in which they function. In this chapter we will take a look at some of the men and women in the early Church who are examples of these gift ministries. This will help us to recognize and understand how these ministries function in the Church today.

First we will look at the process of development whereby a person is recognized as having one of these gift ministries to the Body. To become a prophet, for example, takes a process of growth. It is like growing up an oak tree. Before we see the acorns on a fully developed tree, there has usually been years of maturing from the original seedling.

There are five major steps in the process of development: 1) being a servant first, 2) the calling, 3) answering the call, 4) a period of training, and 5) ordination. The foundation of every minister's life is that he is a servant first. The apostle Paul is a good example of this.

Romans 1:1:
Paul, a servant of Jesus Christ, called to be an apostle, separated unto the gospel of God,

Before Paul is called as an apostle, he said he was a servant. This word in Greek is *doulos*, meaning a bond-slave. Everyone can be a servant like this, but not everyone chooses to be. There is a desire to dedicate one's life to be a servant of the Lord Jesus Christ. It is like saying, "Yes, I will," every time there is an opportunity to serve. A *doulos* type of servant is one who has made a commitment to do everything and anything that the master needs to have done. Epaphras, a man from Colossae, is also called a *doulos.*

Colossians 4:12:
Epaphras, who is one of you, a servant of Christ, saluteth you, always labouring fervently for you in prayers, that ye may stand perfect and complete in all the will of God.

The second step is the calling. This is totally God's prerogative and choosing. A person could desire to be a teacher for example and could even be adept at teaching (because it is one of the functions that every believer can do), but that does not make his life a gift ministry to the Body. That is God's calling of him. Romans 1 explains this as we read before.

Romans 1:1 (ESV):
Paul, a servant of Christ Jesus, called to be an apostle, set apart for the gospel of God,

Paul did not decide to be an apostle. God called him to be one and appointed, or set him apart, for this purpose.

The third step is that the person must answer the call. That is completely the freewill choice of the individual. In God's foreknowledge, he knows who will answer and who will not, but he completely leaves it up to the person to respond to the calling.

Romans 11:29:
For the gifts and calling of God are without repentance.

The gift of the Spirit is given to each believer and God never takes it away, even if the person does not want to recognize it and walk by it. It is the same with the calling of a minister. The calling is not ever withdrawn, no matter what age the person is. I have seen many people begin to be ministers, then take some years away (doing whatever!) and then return to pick up exactly where they were those years before. Obviously, it is God's will that a person be dedicated over their whole life, but God never withdraws the calling.

The fourth step involves a period of learning and training. Becoming a gift minister does not happen overnight. I believe that it is up to those ministers who are already ordained to begin to recognize and encourage a person who is a "fledgling" in these areas and to train them and mentor them. There are many foundational truths that are important to learn and develop and the biggest one is to learn what it means to be a servant. Many people end up influencing a person's life—remember his whole life is the gift to the Body—so it is a unique combination of his talents, abilities, as well as experiences. The joy for ministers is to notice that another person has a desire, has said "Yes," and then to encourage the unfolding of that energizing for the Body.

This learning and training is key to the development of the person's life. Even the apostle Paul had a period of time when he was learning and growing between the time he was called on the road to Damascus and when he actually began ministering in the Body at Antioch. First he spent some period of time in the desert in Arabia, where I believe that Jesus Christ personally taught him, and then with this time, he spent a total of three years in Damascus with the believers there.

Galatians 2:11, 12:
But I certify you, brethren, that the gospel which was preached of me is not after man.
For I neither received it of man, neither was I taught it, but by the revelation of Jesus Christ.

Galatians 1:15-19:
But when it pleased God, who separated me from my mother's womb, and called me by his grace,
To reveal his Son in me, that I might preach him among the heathen; immediately I conferred not with flesh and blood:
Neither went I up to Jerusalem to them which were apostles before me; but I went into Arabia, and returned again unto Damascus.
Then after three years I went up to Jerusalem to see Peter, and abode with him fifteen days.
But other of the apostles saw I none, save James the Lord's brother.

After these three years, Paul went to Jerusalem for fifteen days, but only saw Peter and James, the Lord's brother. The Jews became very angry with him when they found out he was in Jerusalem so the believers took Paul and sent him to Tarsus, away from Jerusalem. Then Paul spent some further time in Tarsus before Barnabas came to ask him to come to Antioch, probably for at least another three years.

Once Paul came to Antioch, he worked very closely with Barnabas and the other ministers there for a year. He is appointed with Barnabas to take a financial gift to Jerusalem during the famine in 43-44 A.D. The first missionary journey with Barnabas took place in 45 A.D., but on this journey he witnessed mostly to Jews, not the Gentiles. It is not until the second missionary journey that the prophecy about being an apostle to the Gentiles starts to come into bold fruition. In Paul's own description of his conversion, he tells the unfolding of his calling:

Acts 26:15-20:

And I said, Who art thou, Lord? And he said, I am Jesus whom thou persecutest.

But rise, and stand upon thy feet: for I have appeared unto thee for this purpose, to make thee a minister and a witness both of these things which thou hast seen, and of those things in the which I will appear unto thee;

Delivering thee from the people, and from the Gentiles, unto whom now I send thee,

To open their eyes, and to turn them from darkness to light, and from the power of Satan unto God, that they may receive forgiveness of sins, and inheritance among them which are sanctified by faith that is in me.

Whereupon, O king Agrippa, I was not disobedient unto the heavenly vision:

But shewed first unto them of Damascus, and at Jerusalem, and throughout all the coasts of Judaea, and then to the Gentiles, that they should repent and turn to God, and do works meet for repentance.

The last step is that by prophecy and laying on hands, a person is ordained. The word "ordained" can be translated as placed or appointed. There are two aspects of this ordination: 1) it is acknowledged that the person is called to be a gift in the Body and 2) an appointment is made whereby the gift is released into a particular ministry such as teaching or pastoring. This could happen in an informal setting or in a public ceremony.

I Timothy 4:14:
And do not despise the gift that you have that was given to you by
prophecy and by the laying on of the hand of the eldership.

At this point, the servant is established in an office of trust and the fruit of his work can be seen by all in the Body of Christ.

<u>APOSTLES</u>

Other than the twelve original apostles and Paul, and James, the Lord's brother, it is difficult to distinguish who in the first century were apostles. Two unknown men are mentioned in Romans and the King James translation makes it appear as though they are apostles.

Romans 16:7 (KJV):
Salute Andronicus and Junia, my kinsmen, and my
fellowprisoners, who are of note among the apostles, who also were
in Christ before me.

But the Aramaic explains that they were known by the apostles, not that they were apostles. This verse is also used to "prove" that apostles can be women, because Junia can be either a masculine or feminine name.

Romans 16:7 (MGI):
Greet Andronicus and Junia, my brothers, who were captives with
me and are known by the apostles and were in Christ before me.

One reason that I believe it is difficult to see who the true apostles were is that they are sent forth with orders, with specific objectives, often with specific jurisdictions. Their primary purpose is to build unity as we saw in the last chapter. Normally they do not draw attention to themselves, but go about their business.

Paul calls only two other people by a specific phrase, which I believe acknowledges them as apostles. That phrase is "fellow-soldier." The term in Greek literature is given to show a high honor to someone who has the same commission. Paul is using it metaphorically, meaning that they are "strategists" together against the wiles of the devil (Ephesians 6:11). He only calls Epaphroditus, a leader in Philippi and Archippus, a leader in Colossae by this name.

Philippians 2:25:
Yet I supposed it necessary to send to you Epaphroditus, my brother, and companion in labour, and fellowsoldier, but your messenger, and he that ministered to my wants.

The word messenger is the word for apostle, or sent one. The Aramaic translation makes this clearer:

Philippians 2:25 (MGI):
But now, a matter urges me to send Epaphroditus to you, a brother who is a helper and worker with me, but your own apostle and a minister for my need,

Epaphroditus was a leader in Philippi who is particularly described in the epistle to the Philippians. He came to Rome with a financial gift for Paul and took on the hazards of this journey of over 800 miles. Epaphroditus came in person to bring Paul the gift because in that culture it was not possible to send money except by an individual and with considerable trouble. If Paul had been in Philippi, they would have supported him directly.

The Macedonian believers, which include those who lived in Philippi, are used in II Corinthians 8 and 9 as a great example of true open-handed giving.

II Corinthians 8:1-5:
Moreover, brethren, we do you to wit of the grace of God bestowed on the churches of Macedonia;
How that in a great trial of affliction the abundance of their joy and their deep poverty abounded unto the riches of their liberality.
For to their power, I bear record, yea, and beyond their power they were willing of themselves;
Praying us with much intreaty that we would receive the gift, and take upon us the fellowship of the ministering to the saints.
And this they did, not as we hoped, but first gave their own selves to the Lord, and unto us by the will of God.

I think that Epaphroditus was a key minister in promoting and teaching about giving and the model of what the churches should do with giving. He risked his life to come to Paul and became sick in the process of it. Paul sends him back to Philippi with the epistle from Rome to tell the people to honor him greatly because of his service.

Philippians 2:26-30:
For he longed after you all, and was full of heaviness, because that ye had heard that he had been sick.
For indeed he was sick nigh unto death: but God had mercy on him; and not on him only, but on me also, lest I should have sorrow upon sorrow.
I sent him therefore the more carefully, that, when ye see him again, ye may rejoice, and that I may be the less sorrowful.
Receive him therefore in the Lord with all gladness; and hold such in reputation:

Because for the work of Christ he was nigh unto death, not regarding his life, to supply your lack of service toward me.

Archippus is the other man who is called "fellow-soldier." There are not any specific records about him other than in Philemon where it shows that he was a leader in the church that was in Philemon's house.

Philemon 1:2:
And to our beloved Apphia, and Archippus our fellowsoldier, and to the church in thy house:

PROPHETS

Barnabas is often cited as an apostle, but I believe that he was a prophet. His original name was Joses or Joseph, and he was named Barnabas by the apostles (Acts 4:36). Barnabas means "son of consolation" or "son of encouragement." What a prophet does is to speak words of exhortation and encouragement, sometimes with reproof. As we have seen earlier, exhortation is like the "breath of God" which brings life-giving oxygen to the body.

Acts 11:22-24:
Then tidings of these things came unto the ears of the church which was in Jerusalem: and they sent forth Barnabas, that he should go as far as Antioch.
Who, when he came, and had seen the grace of God, was glad, and exhorted them all, that with purpose of heart they would cleave unto the Lord.
For he was a good man, and full of the Holy Ghost and of faith: and much people was added unto the Lord.

Agabus is also listed as a prophet who lived in Jerusalem, but came to Antioch to bring a message about the famine that was coming so that the believers could be prepared for it.

Acts 11:27-30:
And in these days came prophets from Jerusalem unto Antioch.
And there stood up one of them named Agabus, and signified by the Spirit that there should be great dearth throughout all the world: which came to pass in the days of Claudius Caesar.
Then the disciples, every man according to his ability, determined to send relief unto the brethren which dwelt in Judaea:
Which also they did, and sent it to the elders by the hands of Barnabas and Saul.

Agabus is seen later in Acts when Paul is on the way to Jerusalem. He prophesies to Paul that he should not go there.

Acts 21:10-12:
And as we tarried there many days, there came down from Judaea a certain prophet, named Agabus.
And when he was come unto us, he took Paul's girdle, and bound his own hands and feet, and said, Thus saith the Holy Ghost, So shall the Jews at Jerusalem bind the man that owneth this girdle, and shall deliver him into the hands of the Gentiles.
And when we heard these things, both we, and they of that place, besought him not to go up to Jerusalem.

EVANGELISTS

Evangelists are preachers, men and women who win people to Christ, as well as heralds of the good news of salvation and deliverance to people who are already believers. Philip was originally one of the seven deacons chosen to help with the food distribution in Jerusalem. This record in Acts 8 takes place in the early days of the persecution against the Christians in Jerusalem before there is any outreach among the Gentiles (approximately 36-37 A.D.). Philip went to Samaria to preach the Word of God and many signs and wonders happened there. Then he is sent to witness to an Ethiopian eunuch.

> *Acts 8:26-30:*
> *And the angel of the Lord spake unto Philip, saying, Arise, and go toward the south unto the way that goeth down from Jerusalem unto Gaza, which is desert.*
> *And he arose and went: and, behold, a man of Ethiopia, an eunuch of great authority under Candace queen of the Ethiopians, who had the charge of all her treasure, and had come to Jerusalem for to worship,*
> *Was returning, and sitting in his chariot read Esaias the prophet.*
> *Then the Spirit said unto Philip, Go near, and join thyself to this chariot.*
> *And Philip ran thither to him, and heard him read the prophet Esaias, and said, Understandest thou what thou readest?*

That is a key question that an evangelist or preacher would ask, "Do you understand what you are reading?" Philip then goes on to preach Christ to him and explain the passage in Isaiah. We run into Philip later in Acts 21, living in Caesarea, having four daughters.

> *Acts 21:8, 9:*
> *And the next day we that were of Paul's company departed, and came unto Caesarea: and we entered into the house of Philip the evangelist, which was one of the seven; and abode with him.*

And the same man had four daughters, virgins, which did prophesy.

The approximate year of the record in Acts 21 is 53 A.D. Philip had spent his whole life being a faithful minister from the early days of the Church. What a great testimony of being steadfast in service!

PASTORS

Pastors are those who tend, help, support and personally care for the believers. One example is a woman of Cenchrea named Phebe who served the Church and ministered to Paul.

Romans 16:1
I commend unto you Phebe our sister, which is a servant of the church which is at Cenchrea:
That ye receive her in the Lord, as becometh saints, and that ye assist her in whatsoever business she hath need of you: for she hath been a succourer of many, and of myself also.

Phebe is called a "succourer," which comes from a Greek word that means a "patroness." Webster's 1828 Dictionary defines a patron as: "an advocate, a defender, one that specially countenances and supports, or lends aid to advance."[22] We might speak of someone who supports a community opera center both financially and promotionally as a patron of the arts. What a beautiful description of this sister Phebe.

---

[22] Webster, Noah. *Noah Webster's First Edition of An American Dictionary of the English Language*, "patron."

Philemon is written by Paul regarding his servant Onesimus. But I think this small epistle shows that Philemon was a wonderful minister who was taking care of the church in his home in Colossae.

Philemon 5-7:
I thank my God, making mention of thee always in my prayers,
Hearing of thy love and faith, which thou hast toward the Lord Jesus, and toward all saints;
That the communication of thy faith may become effectual by the acknowledging of every good thing which is in you in Christ Jesus.
For we have great joy and consolation in thy love, because the bowels of the saints are refreshed by thee, brother.

One of the characteristics of a pastor is that they seek and watch after people that are always wandering or seeming to get lost. They can be a GPS navigational system for some, but also a sanctuary for those who follow them. Philemon refreshed the saints in Colossae with his love and care.

TEACHERS

Before Paul was known and acknowledged as an apostle, he was a teacher. He is listed with the name "Saul" among the first prophets and teachers in Acts 13:1 in Antioch. As his reputation grew in Antioch, it was solidified that he was a prominent teacher. During his first missionary journey with Barnabas, his name was changed from Saul to "Paul" and he was called Paul from that point forward. When they returned to Antioch, there was much to share about the miracles and deliverance that they saw on their trip.

Acts 15:35:
Paul also and Barnabas continued in Antioch, teaching and preaching the word of the Lord, with many others also.

When Paul went to Corinth on his second missionary journey, he ended up staying there for more than a year and a half, teaching the people the Word of God.

Acts 18:8-11:
And Crispus, the chief ruler of the synagogue, believed on the Lord with all his house; and many of the Corinthians hearing believed, and were baptized.
Then spake the Lord to Paul in the night by a vision, Be not afraid, but speak, and hold not thy peace:
For I am with thee, and no man shall set on thee to hurt thee: for I have much people in this city.
And he continued <u>there</u> a year and six months, teaching the word of God among them.

Paul continued to teach and preach throughout his entire life. At the end of Acts, even when he was being held as a prisoner, he was teaching and preaching about the Lord Jesus Christ.

Acts 28:31:
Preaching the kingdom of God, and teaching those things which concern the Lord Jesus Christ, with all confidence, no man forbidding him.

From these brief verses, it is clear that Paul was a teacher first, and then an apostle and perhaps also an evangelist.

Luke is not specifically called a teacher, but I believe that he demonstrates the characteristics of one. He is very interested in the preservation of the Word, and is especially instrumental in gathering together Paul's letters. He is originally a Gentile who travels with Paul on some of his journeys. These are recorded as "we sections" in the book of Acts. Tracing the time in between when he is with Paul, it is apparent that Luke stays in Philippi (and so is there with Epaphroditus) for at least 8 or 9 years. Later he is with Paul in Rome when Paul is writing the epistles of Ephesians, Philippians and Colossians.

CONCLUSION

As we can see from even this brief look at various forerunners in the Body of Christ who served in cities where there were thriving churches, ministers worked together and complemented each other's longsuits. Just as the organs in our physical body work together in the various systems, so do the gift ministries. Epaphroditus, Luke and Silas all spend time in Philippi. Philemon, Archippus and Epaphras all work together in Colossae. If we knew more about the history of the early Church, I am certain it would be more evident regarding who was together with whom. But I think it is clear that the ministers were not isolated in their ministries, but worked together and God called out many men and women to be involved in the care of the believers.

It is also apparent that the title is not important regarding which gift a person is. If it was so vital to know whether a person is a teacher or prophet, then there would be more distinction in the descriptions of their activities. This is where the body analogy breaks down to some extent. An organ cannot change from being a stomach to a lung. However, the way that God designed a man or woman's life to be a gift to the Church, he gave them all the fullness of Christ inside and is constantly energizing that gift in the person. Christ was all five kinds of ministers, so there is the potential that every ordained person can be all five at anytime. In fact, as we grow up into Christ, the overlap of the distinctions between all of the ministries will become less and less. And whatever is needed in the Body at a given time will be energized by God's grace. What a beautiful way for God to have designed the Body of Christ to work that is even more powerful than the physical body!

Chapter 10

JESUS CHRIST, THE HEAD OF THE BODY

Now that we have looked at all of the various parts of the Body of Christ in comparison with the physical body, it is important to put the picture back together in seeing how it works as a unit. The body is a unified whole and cannot function without the head and it cannot function in its various pieces without being a whole unit.

The word in Aramaic for head is *risha*, and has a variety of translations. It can mean a physical head, but when used to represent the head of other things it means, 1) beginning or origination, 2) start or starting point in a series, 3) chief or best part, and 4) ruler or leader. Each of these definitions contributes to our understanding of what it means for Jesus Christ to be head of the Body of Christ.

Colossians 1:18 (MGI):
And he is the head of the body, the church, for he is the beginning and the firstborn from the dead in order that he would be the first in all [things].

The first definition is "beginning." In this verse in Colossians the phrase "beginning and the firstborn" is a figure of speech, *hendiadys*, where two nouns are used, but one thing meant. We noted this figure of speech earlier. When we put the two words together, the phrase could be translated "firstborn leader." Jesus Christ is the eldest son in the family of God and thus he is the leader, or shows the beginning of the Father's relationships with his children. The definition of "beginning" means that there is a point of origin. *Risha* is used in this way in Mark 1.

JESUS CHRIST, THE HEAD OF THE BODY

Mark 1:1:
The beginning of the gospel of Jesus Christ, the Son of God;

The gospel of Mark begins with the ministry of John the Baptist and lines up with the purpose of Mark in revealing Jesus as the servant. Calling Jesus Christ the "beginning and firstborn" reveals him as the starting point of the family of God. He is the eldest son and was born in a unique fashion. Every other son and daughter of God is born by God's Spirit also and is filled with the same measure that was given to Jesus Christ.

The second definition is "starting point of a series." This is similar to the first definition, but it points out that there is a series in which there is a "first." How is Jesus Christ the "first" in the Body of Christ? In the previously quoted verse from Colossians 1:18, he is firstborn from the dead. He is the first of a series of people who will not be subject to death. He is also the "captain" of salvation, meaning the founder and starting point of deliverance for mankind.

Hebrews 2:10:
For it became him, for whom are all things, and by whom are all things, in bringing many sons unto glory, to make the captain of their salvation perfect through sufferings.

Jesus Christ is also the author of faith or the originator of the kind of faith or believing that all believers may have now. He started this trust and reliance on God and has given it to us as part of the gift of Holy Spirit.

Hebrews 12:2 (MGI):
And we should look at Jesus, who was the initiator and finisher of our faith, who for the joy there was for him endured the cross and

discounted the shame and sat down at the right hand of the throne of God.

Not only did he start the first faith and trust as a child of God, but he also completed it so that there is no need for any more faith. We have the faith of Jesus Christ–it is already ours!

Romans 3:22:
Even the righteousness of God which is by faith of Jesus Christ unto all and upon all them that believe: for there is no difference:

The third definition of *risha* is "chief or best part." It indicates the most important or highest ranking one of a group. The Aramaic translation of Mark 12:39 talks about the "chief seats in the synagogues and the chief places at banquets" meaning the most important places. When used in architectural terms, the scriptures call Jesus Christ the head of the corner of the building.

Acts 4:11, 12:
This is the stone which was set at nought of you builders, which is become the head of the corner.
Neither is there salvation in any other: for there is none other name under heaven given among men, whereby we must be saved.

The cornerstone of a building sets the dimensions and framework for the whole building. It sets the angles and it is the most important stone, for the rest of the building is built on it. Salvation is dependent on all that Jesus the Messiah did and accomplished for us and there is no life outside of him.

Ephesians 2:20-22:
And are built upon the foundation of the apostles and prophets, Jesus Christ himself being the chief corner stone;

In whom all the building fitly framed together groweth unto an
holy temple in the Lord:
In whom ye also are builded together for an habitation of God
through the Spirit.

The Aramaic of verse 20 is literally, he is "the head of the corner
of the building." The whole building is framed together, built on
the foundation stone of Jesus Christ. The purpose of the building
is to be a dwelling place of God!

The last definition of *risha* is that of "ruler" or "leader." This
definition is the primary usage of head when describing Jesus
Christ's relationship to the Church.

Ephesians 1:22 (MGI):
And he subjected everything under his feet and he gave him who is
higher than all [to be] the head of the church,
which is his body and the fullness of him who is filling all in all[1]

This definition is used as head or chief in the sense of rank or
authority. Jesus has authority over all things of the Church. The
emphasis in this verse is that **him** who is higher than all has
authority.

Ephesians 4:15, 16 (MGI):
But we should be steadfast in our love, so that [in] everything we
ourselves may grow up in Christ, who is the head.
And from him the whole body is fit together and is knit together in
all the joints, according to the gift that is given by measure to each
member for the growth of the body, that its building up would be
accomplished in love.

JESUS CHRIST, THE HEAD OF THE BODY

We are held closely together as a building and as a Body because of the leadership and authority of Jesus Christ. The words in Greek for "fit together" in Ephesians 4:16 are the same as the words "fitly framed together" from Ephesians 2:21 above.

Colossians 2:19 (ESV):
and not holding fast to the Head, from whom the whole body, nourished and knit together through its joints and ligaments, grows with a growth that is from God.

In conclusion, as a physical body cannot function without a head to guide it, neither can the Body of Christ function without the leadership and headship of Jesus Christ. As our big brother and the firstborn Son, he is the beginning of all of our relationships with God as the Father. He is the starting point of all deliverance and salvation. He is the chief part of the Body and sets the foundation of all its dimensions. And he is the leader and head authority of all functions in the Body of Christ.

Chapter 10

THE BODY TEMPERED TOGETHER

Throughout this book, we have been looking at various parts of the physical body and seeing the comparisons with the Body of Christ. In this concluding chapter we will look at the Body of Christ as a whole unit and see that each of the individual parts cannot function without the others. The explanation of this is vividly laid out in I Corinthians 12:12-27 and we will study this passage in detail.

I Corinthians 12:12-14:
For as the body is one, and hath many members, and all the members of that one body, being many, are one body: so also is Christ.
For by one Spirit are we all baptized into one body, whether we be Jews or Gentiles, whether we be bond or free; and have been all made to drink into one Spirit.
For the body is not one member, but many.

An individual is like a cell or member of the body. This is the great Mystery, that each person has the same Spirit. But the Body of Christ is not just one individual, but many. It takes all the "many" to enable it to be called a Body.

I Corinthians 12:15-18:
If the foot shall say, Because I am not the hand, I am not of the body; is it therefore not of the body?
And if the ear shall say, Because I am not the eye, I am not of the body; is it therefore not of the body?
If the whole body were an eye, where were the hearing? If the whole were hearing, where were the smelling?

91

But now hath God set the members every one of them in the body, as it hath pleased him.

The foot and the hand are combinations of various forms of tissues or cell groups as we have seen. The foot cannot be called a foot unless you look at the framework of bones, tissues, muscles and ligaments. So the tissues do not function without the framework of truth, grace and love. Also, the unique combination of all the parts of the eye allows it to do some specific things. Here is a picture of an eye:

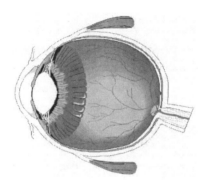

The eye is an amazingly complex organ that performs a very specific function. It is the same with the hearing organ of the ear. Here is a picture of the ear:

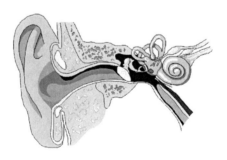

What would we do without the ear or the eye? Even though it is unique in its function, it still requires the whole body in order to function. The sensory impulses need to be communicated back through the nervous system to the brain and thus then communicated throughout the whole body.

I Corinthians 12:19-21:
And if they were all one member, where were the body?
But now are they many members, yet but one body.
And the eye cannot say unto the hand, I have no need of thee: nor again the head to the feet, I have no need of you.

We cannot say to any part of the Body of Christ, "I have no need of you." Every single function, every type of person, every group is necessary for how the Church is to live together and represent Christ. If my eye said to my hand, "I can do your job better. You don't know what is going on," I would not be typing this manuscript. So in the Body of Christ we cannot say to any other part that we do not have need of them.

I Corinthians 12:22-24 (MGI):
But more, there is a necessity for those members that are thought to be weak.
And to those that we think are despised in the body, we give more honor. And for those that are modest, we make more decoration.
Now those members that we have that are honored do not require honor. For God has joined together the body and he has given more honor to the member who is least,

An example of a member of the Body of Christ that is weak is a child. The youngest child in the Church should be held in honor. Why? Because the example of the simple trusting faith of a child is the epitome of how every believer should be.

> *Matthew 18:2-5:*
> *And Jesus called a little child unto him, and set him in the midst of them,*
> *And said, Verily I say unto you, Except ye be converted, and become as little children, ye shall not enter into the kingdom of heaven.*
> *Whosoever therefore shall humble himself as this little child, the same is greatest in the kingdom of heaven.*
> *And whoso shall receive one such little child in my name receiveth me.*

The child realizes that he cannot take care of himself. We would do well to humble ourselves and have a child-like faith. Being the greatest preacher or the greatest miracle worker does not determine a person's greatness in God's eyes. But humility and trust is a key to pleasing him.

The King James version uses a phrase in I Corinthians 12:24 that explains how the Body of Christ is supposed to fit together.

> *I Corinthians 12:24, 25:*
> *For our comely parts have no need: but God hath tempered the body together, having given more abundant honour to that part which lacked:*
> *That there should be no schism in the body; but that the members should have the same care one for another.*

The word "tempered" is the Greek word, *sugkerannumi,* and is a very interesting word. Its basic meaning is to mix together. Regarding the Body of Christ, it means that God has caused the several parts to unite into a whole in an organic structure. The emphasis is not on the parts, but on the whole. The only other place that this word is used is in Hebrews.

> *Hebrews 4:2:*
> *For unto us was the gospel preached, as well as unto them: but the word preached did not profit them, not being mixed with faith in them that heard it.*

Clarke's Commentary is particularly vivid in his explanation of the use of this word *sugkerannumi*:

> *The word συγκεκραμενος, mixed, is peculiarly expressive; it is a metaphor taken from the nutrition of the human body by mixing the aliment taken into the stomach with the saliva and gastric juice, in consequence of which it is concocted, digested, reduced into chyle, which, absorbed by the lacteal vessels, and thrown into the blood, becomes the means of increasing and supporting the body, all the solids and fluids being thus generated; so that on this process, properly performed, depend (under God) strength, health, and life itself. Should the most nutritive aliment be received into the stomach, if not mixed with the above juices, it would be rather the means of death than of life; or, in the words of the apostle, it would not profit, because not thus mixed. Faith in the word preached, in reference to that God who sent it,[23]*

The emphasis is that with the mixture, there is profit. Hebrews is in the context of faith, but I Corinthians 12 is talking about how the Body of Christ works together so that there would be no schism. All the parts are necessary! And not only that, they work

---

[23] Clarke, Adam, *The New Testament of our Lord and Saviour Jesus Christ, Commentary on the Bible*, p. 709.

together to form an organic whole that produces more than the individual parts. In the book, *The Church Which is His Body*, by Henry Howard, he summarizes the integration of the individuals in the Body of Christ as follows: "It is literally a banding or binding together of mutually related parts, each of which can retain its own individuality or specialization only as association with its fellows is sustained."[24]

An additional idea of this word "tempered" is that not only is there a mixing or mingling, but that there is a mutual adjustment to one another. This is vividly seen when believers of various groups work closely together and begin to depend and rely upon each other's strengths. There is an acknowledgment that the sum of the parts is greater than the individual part by itself.

A few years ago, five of the leaders here in San Diego began to work together to develop a youth leadership training program. The initial planning meetings were quite interesting because of our different viewpoints. What happened as a result of "mixing" our perspectives together was a program that had a much greater variety and we were able to meet the needs of the youth in a broader and more exciting way. There was a "mutual adjustment" that happened in working together with each other. We grew individually and together and there was a positive impact on the youth. Our combined viewpoints and perspectives enhanced the topics we developed and taught.

I believe that this word "tempered" summarizes the way that the Body of Christ should work together. And it summarizes the various elements of this book. We each may be an individual

---

[24] Howard, Henry, *The Church Which is His Body*, Studied in the Light of Biological Research, p. 27.

member in the Church, but without the other members and without being tempered together with each other, the whole Body will not function properly.

> *I Corinthians 12:25-27 (MGI):*
> *so that there would not be division in the body, but rather [that] all the members would care for one another equally,*
> *so that when one member was hurt, all of them would suffer, and if one member was praised, all the members would be praised.*
> *Now you are the body of Christ and members in your place.*

The purpose of the tempering together is that the members would care for each other equally and appreciate all that each person offers in the Body. One cell by itself does not accomplish that much. Each one is necessary, but combined with other "members," it can accomplish a lot of things.

SUMMARY

> *I Corinthians 12:27:*
> *Now ye are the body of Christ, and members in particular.*

The metaphor that "ye are the body of Christ" is so powerful! When we read "ye" in the King James Version, it mean you (plural), working together, loving together, living together, preaching together. We together magnify the awesome wisdom of God in placing us as particular members which make up an organic functioning unit. The picture of the body in all its various parts, cells, tissues, organs and systems offers startling and thought-provoking comparisons regarding how the Body of Christ functions.

THE BODY TEMPERED TOGETHER

There are two main points that have surfaced throughout this book. One is that no matter what kind of "cell" you are in the Body of Christ, you are important and you should function in what God has called you to do and be and it will work together with all the rest of the believers in the Church. The second point is that when you are willing to serve in the Church and continue to say, "Yes" to the leading of the Lord Jesus Christ within, you will grow in grace, and your calling and ministry will be apparent to the whole Body.

Ephesians 4:15:
But speaking the truth in love, may grow up into him in all things, which is the head, even Christ:

Christ in you is the mystery of the one Body. We each have the same measure of the Spirit. No matter where we came from or what we have done, we each have a special "particular" part in the Body of Christ, the Church. So let us all get busy "growing up into him" and living in the fullness of the mystery today!

Bibliography

Barker, Kenneth, et al. *The NIV Study Bible*. Grand Rapids, Michigan: Zondervan Publishing House, 1995.

Barnes, Charles Randall, ed. *The People's Bible Encyclopedia*. Chicago: The People's Publication Society, 1921.

Brown, Francis, S.R. Driver, Charles A. Briggs, eds. *The New Brown-Driver-Briggs-Gesenius Hebrew and English Lexicon*. Christian Copyrights, Inc., 1983.

Brown, Raymond E., Joseph A. Fitzmyer, Roland E. Murphy. *The Jerome Biblical Commentary*. Englewood Cliffs, New Jersey: Prentice-Hall, Inc., 1968.

Bruun, Ruth Dowling and Bertel. *The Human Body, Your Body and How It Works*. New York: Random House, 1982.

Bullinger, E. W. *A Critical Lexicon and Concordance to the English and Greek New Testament*. Grand Rapids, Michigan: Zondervan Publishing House, 1975.

Bullinger, E.W., *Figures of Speech Used in the Bible*. Grand Rapids, Michigan: Baker Book House, 1968.

Clarke, Adam, *The New Testament of our Lord and Saviour Jesus Christ,* Commentary on the Bible. New York: Abingdon Press. Volumes 1-6.

Douglas, J. D, ed. *New Bible Dictionary*. Wheaton, Illinois: Tyndale House Publishers, 1987.

Ellicott, Charles, ed. *The Layman's Handy Commentary on the Bible, Epistles to the Galatians, Ephesians and Philippians.* Grand Rapids, Michigan: Zondervan Publishing House, 1957.

Gaebelein, Frank E. *The Expositor's Bible Commentary.* Grand Rapids, Michigan: Zondervan Publishing House, 1984.

Goldberg, Stephen, M.D. *Clinical Anatomy Made Ridiculously Simple.* Miami: MedMaster Inc., 1984.

Gray, Henry, *Anatomy, Descriptive and Surgical,* a Revised American. From the Fifteenth English Edition. New York: Bounty Books, 1977.

Harris, R. Laird, Gleason L. Archer, Jr., Bruce K. Waltke, eds. *Theological Wordbook of the Old Testament.* Chicago: Moody Press, 1980. 2 volumes.

Harter, Jim, ed. *Anatomical and Medical Illustrations.* Mineola, New York: Dover Publications, Inc. 1991.

Howard, Henry, *The Church Which is His Body,* Studied in the Light of Biological Research. London: The Epworth Press, 1923.

Jacobus, Melancthon W. and Elbert C. Lane, Andrew C. Zenos, ed. *Funk & Wagnall's New Standard Bible Dictionary.* Garden City, New York: Garden City Books, 1936.

Jennings, William. *Lexicon to the Syriac New Testament.* London: Oxford University Press, 1926.

Lamsa, George M. *Gospel Light, A Revised Annotated Edition.* Aramaic Bible Society, 1999.

Lightfoot, John. *A Commentary on the New Testament from the Talmud and Hebraica. 4 vols.* Peabody, Massachusetts: Hendrickson Publishers, 1989.

Marieb, Elaine N. *Essentials of Human Anatomy & Physiology.* Redwood City, California: The Benjamin/Cummings Publishing Company, Inc., 1984.

Milligan, G. and Moulton, J.H. *Vocabulary of the Greek New Testament.* Peabody, Massachusetts: Hendrickson Publishers, 1997.

Moffatt, James. *A New Translation of the Bible.* New York: Harper & Row, Publishers, 1954.

Murdock, James, trans. *The New Testament.* New York: Stanford and Swords, 1852.

Murray, John. *The New International Commentary on the New Testament,* The Epistle to the Romans. Grand Rapids, Michigan: Wm. B. Eerdmans Publishing Co., 1990.

Nave, Orville J. *The New Nave's Topical Bible.* Grand Rapids, Michigan: Zondervan Publishing House, 1969.

Nicoll, W. Robertson, ed. *The Expositor's Greek New Testament.* Grand Rapids, Michigan: William B. Eerdmans Publishing Co., 1970. 5 volumes.

BIBLIOGRAPHY

Rice, Edwin W. *People's Dictionary of the Bible*. Philadelphia: American Sunday-School Union, 1904.

Ryken, Leland, ed. *Dictionary of Biblical Imagery*. Downers Grove, Illinois: InterVarsity Press, 1998.

Scanlon, Valerie C. and Sander, Tina. *Essentials of Anatomy and Physiology*. Philadelphia: F.A. Davis Company, 1991.

Schade, Johannes P. *Introduction to Functional Human Anatomy, an Atlas*. Philadelphia: W.B. Saunders Company, 1974.

Smith, J. Payne. *A Compendious Syriac Dictionary*. London: Oxford at the Clarendon Press, 1967.

Thayer, Joseph Henry. *The New Thayer's Greek-English Lexicon of the New Testament*. Christian Copyrights, Inc., 1981.

Vannini, Vanio and Pogliani, Giuliano, *The Color Atlas of Human Anatomy*. New York: Harmony Books, 1994.

Vincent, Marvin R. *Word Studies in the New Testament*. Grand Rapids, Michigan: Wm. B. Eerdmans Publishing Co., 1946. 4 volumes.

Wagner, C. Peter, *Finding Your Spiritual Gifts*. Oxnard, California: Gospel Light Publications, 2005.

Webster, Noah, *Noah Webster's first Edition of An American Dictionary of the English Language*. San Francisco: Foundation for American Christian Education, 1967.

BIBLIOGRAPHY

Webster's New World Dictionary of the American Language. Cleveland: The World Publishing Company, 1956.

Welch, Charles, *The Testimony of the Lord's Prisoner.* London: The Berean Publishing Trust, 1931.

Wilson, Mitchell, *The Human Body, What It Is and How It Works.* New York: Golden Press, 1959.

About the Author

Janet Magiera is an ordained minister and has been serving in the Body of Christ for over 30 years. From the late 1970's when she studied Aramaic with a student of Dr. George Lamsa, she has continued to search for understanding of the scriptures through Eastern customs, figures of speech and the study of the Biblical languages. This has culminated in the last few years with the publication of a library of books for use in studying the Aramaic Peshitta New Testament.

She and her husband Glen founded Light of the Word Ministry in 1998. Jan continues to teach in various fellowships and churches around the nation. Her first book, *Enriched in Everything*, is a study on the Biblical principles of giving. Jan's ability to sift through difficult topics and to present them in a thought-provoking and articulate manner is evident in this book also.

Glen and Jan currently live in San Diego, California and work together with San Diego Biblical Studies Fellowship.

Books by Janet M. Magiera
Gospel Light (editor)
Enriched in Everything
Aramaic Peshitta New Testament Translation
Parallel Translations
Vertical Interlinear, Vol I, II, III
Word Study Concordance
Dictionary Lexicon